WADSWORTH PHILOSOPHERS SERIES

D0470212

ON

HUME

Elizabeth S. Radcliffe
Santa Clara University

Wadsworth
Thomson Learning

Australia • Canada • Mexico • Singapore • Spain
United Kingdom • United States

Printed in the United States of America
1 2 3 4 5 6 7 03 02 01 00 99

For permission to use material from this text, contact us:
Web: http://www.thomsonrights.com
Fax: 1-800-730-2215
Phone: 1-800-730-2214

For more information, contact:
Wadsworth/Thomson Learning
10 Davis Drive
Belmont, CA 94002-3098
USA
http://www.wadsworth.com

ISBN: 0-534-57605-2

Contents

Preface

I give citations to the following works by Hume in the text of this book, rather than in footnotes, using the abbreviations below. Citations in the text include page number(s) from the listed edition.

T   *A Treatise of Human Nature*, ed. by L.A. Selby-Bigge, 2nd ed. revised by P.H. Nidditch (Oxford University Press, 1978).

EHU   *An Enquiry Concerning Human Understanding*, ed. by L.A. Selby-Bigge, 3rd ed. revised by P.H. Nidditch (Oxford University Press, 1975). ["The first *Enquiry*"]

EPM   *An Enquiry Concerning the Principles of Morals*, ed. by L.A. Selby-Bigge, 3rd ed. revised by P.H. Nidditch (Oxford University Press, 1975). ["The second *Enquiry*"]

DNR   *Dialogues Concerning Natural Religion*, ed. By Richard H. Popkin (Hackett Publishing, 1980).

My treatment of Hume's theory of ideas and of his analysis of causality in chapters 1 and 2 draws from both the *Enquiry Concerning Human Understanding* and *A Treatise of Human Nature*. The reader may notice a sudden absence of references to the *Enquiry* in Chapter 3; Hume chose not to deal with the difficult topics of the world and the self in that book. My discussions of the passions and of morality, in chapters 4 and 5, largely follows the *Treatise* (with a few references to the second *Enquiry*), and the final chapter, on religion, relies upon the *Dialogues Concerning Natural Religion* and the first *Enquiry*. I regret that I don't have the space in this text to argue for my interpretations of Hume on various points, and there is much excellent contemporary scholarship to which I cannot refer. I only hope my presentation is a stimulus to good discussion over the major themes in the work of my favorite philosopher. I thank Kenneth Winkler for commenting on the first three chapters of this book, and Rick McCarty for reading and commenting on an entire draft of the manuscript more than once.

1

Pushing his Fortune
as a Philosopher:
A Theory of Ideas

The biographer E.C. Mossner quotes David Hume, the Scottish Enlightenment thinker, who was writing in the last months of his life to his publisher: "I remember an Author, who says, that one half of a man's life is too little to write a Book: and the other half to correct it."[1] Hume reworked one of his favorite books, his *Dialogues Concerning Natural Religion*, until the end of his life, knowing that its posthumous publication would capture a mixed audience of admirers and critics. Hume is undoubtedly the most influential philosopher in the tradition of British empiricism and scientific naturalism--a tradition emphasizing observation and induction over metaphysical speculation. His views were radical for his time, and he strove hard to convey them to an educated public. Hume's theories continue to command very serious consideration from contemporary philosophers and have exerted a deep and lasting influence on thinking in epistemology, ethics, and religion.

A Life of Ideas

There is a remarkable fit between the way Hume lived his life and the content of his thought. His views on morality emphasized sympathy, "the sentiment of humanity," and traits useful and agreeable to the self and to others. Hume himself is described as a man of a kind

1

and amiable disposition, who, despite the misfortunes of a writer's life--having his best work ignored and having his ideas used to deny him a university position--retained his equanimity all of his life. He is said to have reasoned himself out of religious belief.[2] When confronted on his deathbed by James Boswell, who hoped to extract a personal confession about secret hopes for an afterlife, Hume displayed a calm demeanor and kept his intellectual integrity. True to his earlier conclusions, he could only say that, however pleasant the thought that he might again see his friends, he had no reason to believe such a thing were possible. He was also aware of the sometimes-odd tension between philosophy and ordinary life, and so expressed in his writing the need to emerge from the abstruse thinking of the study to become involved in the social affairs of common life. Readers are fond of quoting his advice: "Be a philosopher; but, amidst all your philosophy, be still a man" (EHU 9).

Early Life

David Hume was born in Edinburgh, Scotland, on April 26, 1711, to the lawyer Joseph Home and Home's wife and stepsister, Katherine Falconer. (David later changed the spelling of his surname to match its pronunciation.) David, along with an older brother and sister, had a pleasant childhood, although not one of great financial wealth, on the family estate at Ninewells. The children were raised by their hard-working mother, who was left with three children after the death of her husband in 1713. Hume himself reports to have developed a "passion" for literature very early in life.[3] As a boy he took religion very seriously and extracted a list of vices from the 18th-century devotional book, *The Whole Duty of Man*, with which he challenged himself. Among the vices noted there were: "not arranging any solemn time for humiliation and confession," "making pleasure, not health, the end of eating," and "wasting the time or estate in good fellowship."[4]

Despite expectations that David would be a lawyer, he was not to follow in the profession of his father. Hume was drawn to the life of a philosopher early on, after four years of formal study at the University of Edinburgh, which he began at age 11 or 12, and after several years of subsequent independent study. During this time of reading and learning, he studied law, literature and philosophy. He writes, "The Law, which was the Business I design'd to follow, appear'd nauseous to me, & I could think of no other way of pushing my Fortune in the

World, but that of a Scholar & Philosopher."[5] While engaged in this independent reflection, Hume formulated the empiricist views for which he was to become famous, but he also developed a lingering depression. He was diagnosed by a doctor as having "the disease of the learned." The prescribed remedy was anti-hysteric pills and bitters, a daily pint of claret, and exercise. But Hume knew that he shared an affliction with other thinkers who were tormented by persistent, serious contemplation of humanity and its condition. In 1734, after four years of coping with the illness, when he was finally on the road to recovery, Hume went to France to find a country retreat. He settled at LaFleche and frequented the Jesuit college, where the famous French philosopher, Descartes, had also studied. There, at age 23, he wrote the majority of his most important work, *A Treatise of Human Nature*.

Writings and Mid-Life

A Treatise of Human Nature divides into three books. Book I, "Of the Understanding," and Book II, "Of the Passions," were published together in 1739. Book III, "Of Morals," appeared in 1940. The public reception of the *Treatise* was a huge disappointment; Hume says, "It fell *dead-born from the Press*."[6] Actually, some people did read it, but often misunderstood it, and the book did not sell well. The even-tempered Hume bounced back from his letdown, however, and in 1742, put out two volumes of essays, called "*Essays Moral and Political*," written in the spirit of the philosophy of the *Treatise*. The *Essays* were a public success.

Two years later, Hume applied for the vacant chair in Ethics and Spiritual Philosophy at the University of Edinburgh. His views in the previously ignored *Treatise* were now more widely known. Hume was regarded as a skeptic, an atheist, and a humanist: He thought that we can know nothing about the world outside the mind; that religious belief is unfounded; and that morality is dependent on human sentiment, not on God's laws. The tide of popular opinion and much of the professorate went against Hume's appointment. Francis Hutcheson, who occupied the Glasgow Chair of Moral Philosophy from 1729 until his death in 1746, was a friend and correspondent of Hume, but he was also opposed to the appointment. Hutcheson himself was apparently a scintillating lecturer and was said to make the students "relish" virtue and to "pant to be what they beheld".[7] Ironically, the Town Council elected Hutcheson, and not Hume, to the Edinburgh Chair, but he declined it. David Hume never held a university chair.

3

For the next few years, Hume had a couple of jobs. He worked as tutor to the flamboyant and unstable Marquis of Annandale, and as secretary to General James St. Clair, a distant relative planning a later-unsuccessful invasion of French Canada. Some time in this interval, Hume had reworked the first book of his unsuccessful *Treatise* into a presentation he thought more fit for popular reading. His now influential *Enquiry Concerning Human Understanding* was published in 1748. His rewriting of Treatise Book III, *Enquiry Concerning the Principles of Morals*, came in 1751. In the years 1752-1765, Hume was elected Chair of Edinburgh's Philosophical Society, but was denied the Chair of Logic at Glasgow University. He was appointed Keeper of the Advocates' Library, Edinburgh, and subsequently published *The History of England* in six volumes, from 1754-62. The first volume, in which he tried to be politically neutral, got a cold reception, and Hume writes of his great discouragement:

> I thought, I was the only Historian, that had at once neglected present Power, Interest, and Authority, and the Cry of Popular Prejudices; and as the Subject was suited to every Capacity, I expected proportional Applause: But miserable was my Disappointment: I was assailed by one Cry of Reproach, Disapprobation, and even Detestation: ...
>
> I was . . . I confess, discouraged; and had not the War been at that time breaking out between France and England, I had certainly retired to some provincial Town of the former Kingdom, have changed my Name, and never more have returned to my native Country.[8]

The other volumes were published with mixed success, but Hume learned to ignore the fickleness of critical reaction to his writings. He eventually drew a financial profit from his efforts, and within ten years, his *History* was very popular. At age 50, he was determined to stay in Scotland and pursue his literary and philosophical career, but in 1763, he was offered appointment to the position of Secretary to the Embassy in Paris. Upon accompanying the British ambassador there, Hume received a grand reception and remained until 1766. During this time, he fell in love with a Madame de Boufflers, a married woman who was in love with a prince, rather than with David. Hume was deeply loyal to her for the rest of his life, and even while on his deathbed, he wrote her a note of condolence on the death of her beloved Prince de Conte.

Hume's essays on suicide and the immortality of the soul were completed around 1755, and they were printed along with three other essays as part of a book, *Five Dissertations*. But advanced copies stirred a negative reaction among influential readers, so Hume and his printer agreed to physical removal of the two essays from the copies already in print. They were replaced with an essay titled, "Of the Standard of Taste," and the book of essays appeared in 1757 as *Four Dissertations*. The collection included "The Natural History of Religion," which traced the psychological origins of religious belief. Secret copies of the two withdrawn essays appeared anonymously in French (1770) and later, after Hume's death, in English (1777).[9]

Hume's plans for solitary writing time were once again interrupted by an appointment he simply could not refuse. In 1767, Hume accepted an invitation to become under-secretary of state in London. It was not a very comfortable position for him; his sympathies were with the American Colonies: "I am an American in my Principles, and wish we would let them alone to govern or misgovern themselves as they think proper."[10] Still he kept his position until retiring to Edinburgh in 1769. He built a house in St. Andrews Square in Edinburgh, where the American, Ben Franklin, was among his first house guests.

Last Years and Posthumous Controversies

Hume's health started slowly to deteriorate beginning around 1772. He was quite anxious to see to the publication after his death of his *Dialogues Concerning Natural Religion*, which he had written twenty years earlier and revised again in the last months of his life. Hume asked his good friend, Adam Smith, author of *The Wealth of Nations*, to ensure publication of this book after Hume was gone. Given the inflammatory nature of the *Dialogues*, which argued that religious belief was rationally unfounded, Smith was indecisive. Hume feared that his book would not see the light of day, so he also decided to leave copies with one of his publishers and with his nephew, David.

Hume, dying probably of cancer, held a farewell dinner with his friends on July 4, 1776. It is a coincidence that this was also the day of the signing of the American Declaration of Independence in Philadelphia. Hume's biographer notes that, unlike most of his friends, Hume would have rejoiced when the news reached Edinburgh a few days before his death.[11] David kept his tranquility and cheerfulness until the end; he claimed to be no more distressed at the thought of his passing out of existence than he would be at the thought that he had never existed at all. He died on August 25, 1776.

Even in death, David Hume was a source of consternation to both his acquaintances and the public. Adam Smith, probably guilt-ridden over his ambivalence about having the *Dialogues* published, wrote a tribute to Hume. It appeared in a Scottish magazine in 1777, along with Hume's brief autobiography, "My Own Life." Smith was lambasted by pietists who were outraged at Hume's ostensible fearlessness of God and of death. James Boswell, bothered by his last conversation with Hume over the existence of an afterlife, appeared at the cemetery on the day of Hume's funeral, peering first into the dug grave, and then lingering unseen behind a wall. He expressed great anger with Hume, until in 1784, he dreamt of finding Hume's diary. Boswell's emotions were alleviated by his dream "revelations" in which Hume's private religious beliefs and piety were revealed.[12]

In 1779, David's nephew saw to the publication of *The Dialogues Concerning Natural Religion.* In 1783 the two suppressed essays were published with Hume's name attached. Along with the two essays, the anonymous editor of the 1783 edition included his own critical notes to Hume's two pieces, and excerpts from Rousseau's *La Nouvelle Heloise,* on the subject of suicide. The title page read,

ESSAYS ON SUICIDE, AND THE IMMORTALITY OF THE SOUL, ASCRIBED TO THE LATE DAVID HUME, Esq. Never before published. With REMARKS, intended as an Antidote to the Poison contained in these Performances, BY THE EDITOR. TO WHICH IS ADDED, TWO LETTERS ON SUICIDE, FROM ROUSSEAU'S ELOISA.[13]

Little did Hume's acquaintances and relatives realize the legacy Hume had left to the philosophical world.

A Theory of Ideas

Hume's project in *A Treatise of Human Nature* is to implement the newly developed scientific method in an empirical study of human nature. In his Introduction to the *Treatise* and also in the abstract of that work, a summary that Hume published as an advertisement, he likens his project to that of several contemporaries who have applied the methods of the 17th-century natural philosopher, Francis Bacon, to "the science of man."[14] Bacon was a key figure in the evolution of the modern scientific method, because he incorporated a balance of

6

observation and reasoning in his study of natural phenomena and recognized the possibility of fallacious thinking due to social and personal biases. Hume is interested in a similarly empirical, objective, and reasoned study, but applied to three aspects of human nature--the understanding, the passions, and morality.

Hume's project is unique in its scope and rigor as compared to the work of the predecessors he acknowledges. John Locke, for instance, develops an empiricist theory of the origin of ideas that he presents as the basis of all knowledge. Yet, his analysis does not undertake a deep systematic study of the emotions, and his treatment of our knowledge of the external world at times lacks rigor. Francis Hutcheson, on the other hand, offers an analysis of the passions and of our "moral sense," but he multiplies principles of explanation beyond credibility. Hume's philosophy is a comprehensive philosophy of mind. His aim is to say definitively, in as few principles as possible, what moral beings, who act and who are the subjects of moral judgment, can know and how they can be moved. In order to address these issues, Hume begins with a study of the contents of the mind, since anything human beings know and do must ultimately depend on what occurs mentally. Any certainty we have depends on our present experience, to which we have immediate, direct access, and any motives we have depend on those mental states, which urge us to action.

Impressions and Ideas

Hume calls any content of the mind a "perception." He writes in the opening lines of the *Treatise*,

> ALL the perceptions of the human mind resolve themselves into two distinct kinds, which I shall call IMPRESSIONS and IDEAS. The difference betwixt these consists in the degree of force and liveliness, with which they strike upon the mind, and make their way into our thought or consciousness (T 1).

Impressions are the vivid and forceful experiences we have when we see, hear, taste, smell, or touch, or when we feel passions such as love, pride, envy, or desire. Ideas, on the other hand, are the less vivid and less lively mental states we have when we think about the original ones. For instance, my perceptions of a rose garden as I walk through it are different in quality from the mental contents I have as later I think of the rose garden after I've left it. Hume says that even though splendid

7

poetry may evoke ideas of a colorful landscape, "The most lively thought is still inferior to the dullest sensation" (EHU 17). Likewise, being in love and thinking of being love, or being in pain and thinking of being in pain, feel quite different to the subject of the perceptions.

Hume calls the perceptions of colors, tastes, odors, sounds, textures, pleasures, pains, and so on, "impressions of sensation." He calls the emotions (or passions) "impressions of reflection,"[15] since our emotions are evoked when we reflect upon the sources of our pleasures and pains. I take pleasure in your company; when I realize that fact, an affection or liking for you arises in me, and that affection is an impression because of its forceful experiential quality. Note, then, that passions are not ideas, even though they occur after reflection. They are *vivid and forceful* experiences, which arise when we think about something that has felt pleasurable or painful. They are separate from the *thought* of the pleasure or the pain, which is an idea. To understand Hume's project is to understand why he distinguishes the contents of the mind solely on the grounds of their phenomenal "feel," how they feel to us, rather than by the supposed mental processes or external objects that might be the causes of the perceptions: We are immediately aware of the quality of an experience, but not of its cause, whether mental or extramental. So, to begin with something *not* inferred, as an empirical inquiry should, we must start by studying the perceptions themselves.

Is my experience of a pineapple a single impression on Hume's theory? Impressions can be simple or complex. The unique taste of the pineapple and its yellow color are each a simple impression, but when they are conjoined with the other impressions of its texture and smell and so on, the group together constitutes the complex impression of a pineapple. Ideas, likewise, are simple or complex, since I can think about a single impression, such as a pineapple-taste, or I can think of the fruit, that is, of all of its qualities together. Hume argues that all of our simple ideas can be traced to previous simple impressions; if I am missing a particular impression, I cannot understand the corresponding idea. Both of these claims are supported by experience, according to Hume. First, try as I may, he believes I can think of no idea not originating in a sensation or a feeling.[16] Second, a person without sight lacks the color concepts with which normally sighted people are conversant; a person without smell lacks the odor concepts the rest of us recognize; and so on, for the other senses. So, it is part of Hume's view that mental contents are never innate, or in the mind at birth.

None of this is to rule out the possibility of our having ideas of the imagination, as long as the imagination is understood properly, as

8

limited by sensory input. I can imagine a winged horse because I have experienced a horse at some time and wings (on a bird) at another; but Hume thinks it makes no sense to say I can conjure up an original idea out of no previous mental contents. So, the imagination can detach simple ideas from a complex and recombine them in original ways.

Some readers believe that Hume's theory commits him to a "picture theory" of ideas, the view that every thought is actually a mental image or picture in the mind. Indeed, his own language promotes this understanding, as when he says, for example, that ideas "copy" their impressions and are "resemblances" of them. The picture theory does well to explain how an idea of a color or a shape resembles its origin, since such ideas are visual, and we might say the idea is a fuzzy mental picture of the impression. Yet, we ask, how does an idea of a smell resemble the original experience of it, and how does an idea of a taste copy the impression? Is my thought of the lemon's sour taste qualitatively like my actual tasting of its sourness--can they "feel" similar, when one is sensation and the other conceptualization? Is my thought of pain a diminished version of the feeling itself? The picture theory seems ill suited to explain ideas of these other senses; so, there is at least a puzzle here, trying to explain how ideas are *copies* of impressions, if Hume means to say that they are.

Memory and Imagination

What is it to remember, as opposed to imagine, to sense as opposed to reason? Many philosophers think of the functions of the mind--sense perception, memory, reason, imagination, will, and so forth--in terms of mental "faculties." Faculty psychology has it that the mind's capacities are active powers or processes, which work to produce ideas, beliefs, conclusions, memories, and so on. On this view, the mind is something beyond its own ideas, possessing, as it were, different parts defined by their different functions. Even though Hume, for want of a better term, at times refers to the "faculty" of memory or of imagination, he does not subscribe to a faculty psychology. His is an attempt to avoid the problems of some of his predecessors who, in positing individual faculties, end up with a multiplicity of internal agents engineering the remembering, the reasoning, the imagining, the willing, and so on, for the mind whose processes are being explained.[17] Accordingly, Hume distinguishes memory from imagination, not by the mental processes, but in this way:

9

> We find by experience, that when any impression has been present with the mind, it again makes its appearance there as an idea; and this it may do after two different ways: either when in its new appearance it retains a considerable degree of its first vivacity, and is somewhat intermediate betwixt an impression and an idea; or when it intirely loses that vivacity, and is a perfect idea. The faculty, by which we repeat our impressions in the first manner, is called the MEMORY, and the other the IMAGINATION (T 8-9).

Common reaction, Hume notes, is to reply that memory is distinct from imagination in that the former preserves the order of ideas as they came in experience, while the latter does not. Hume responds that we have no way of applying such a criterion to make the distinction, since we cannot conjure up the past impressions and compare their order to our present ideas. Any attempt to think of past impressions necessarily has us considering them as ideas. In other words, we would need to know already that we are recalling our experiences in the proper order in order to determine whether we are properly recalling our experiences. So, the order or arrangement of complex ideas cannot tell us whether they are ideas of memory or imagination (T 85).

Thus, Hume turns to the only criterion possible on his theory of ideas: the forcefulness and vivacity of the ideas themselves. On his view, then, impressions (of sensation and reflection) are the most forceful mental states, ideas of memory are less so, and ideas of the imagination even less. Of course, this distinction causes problems, some of which Hume acknowledges himself: Memories fade and we become unsure whether we are remembering or imagining; likewise, thoughts of imagined events, such as those depicted in the lies of a chronic liar, pick up forcefulness and strength the more frequently they are repeated (T 85-86). When the liar begins to believe his own lies, then they must pass from imagination into memory, but we say that can't be so. Furthermore, one contemporary commentator has noted that the sudden realization of a memory can make it strike the mind with a force and vivacity stronger than a present impression. An investigator examines the scene of a crime; later, in her office, when thinking on all that she saw, she is struck suddenly with the memory of something significant to her investigation, which she didn't note at the time--a poker standing on the left side of the fireplace.[18] Obviously, she had a previous experience of the poker, but it didn't strike her then with the forcefulness it has upon returning in her memory. It looks as though some memories are more lively than the preceding impressions, contrary to Hume's claim.

10

Are these problems insurmountable obstacles to Hume's theory of ideas? He thought not, since he points out some of them himself (T 85-86). Also consider the following in Hume's defense. First, the distinction between memory and imagination is a general perplexity, no matter one's philosophical bent: If we make it necessary to memory that it be a mental replication of facts, then we can make no sense of someone's "misremembering" or wrongly remembering some event. If we want to make sense of mistaken memory, then we require a criterion of memory identification that consists in some feature internal to the mental state itself; we are back in Hume's shoes. And the vivid memory example may actually not prove problematic for Hume's theory, either. Hume might respond with a distinction between the idea of a scene and the idea of the significance of a scene. Hume could make the point that the investigator had experience of the impressions which constitute the image of the poker on the left side of the fireplace; at that time, the impressions themselves registered with the vivacity of all color, shape, texture, etc., experiences. While the thought of that scene hit the detective with some forcefulness later, because she then recognized its import in a way she hadn't before, the mere thought of the scene is still an experience dulled in vivacity when compared to the impressions she received of the various objects in the room.

The Association of Ideas

Hume observes that one thought's passing to another occurs not with sheer randomness, but with a discernable regularity. Just as physicists can formulate laws of physics to describe the regularities in nature, Hume offers three principles of the association of ideas, which describe the ways in which the mind moves from one idea to the next. Ideas, he says, are associated by resemblance, contiguity, or cause and effect (T 11). For example, I meet your niece, and, because of resemblance, my idea of her reminds me of you. My thoughts of you pass on to an idea of your best friend, since these two ideas--of you and of your friend--have occurred to me "contiguously" in the past, in close temporal proximity. And from this idea, my mind moves to an idea of your friend's son, who is associated with your friend by causation; she is part of the causal origin of her son.

Hume thinks these principles explain how we come by our ideas of complexes, which divide into three types: relations, substances, and modes (T 13). Relations are the result of comparing one idea to another idea to derive such notions as identity or contrariety (sameness or difference), above or below, and heavier than or lighter than. "Substance" here refers to the class of ideas that are our ideas of objects. We have simple impressions of particular colors, tastes, sounds, odors, and so forth, but we give our complex idea of a group of these an object name. For instance, we call the redness, roundness, sweetness, shininess, and crispness we perceive contiguously, "apple," when we want to attribute these qualities to a common cause. We form the complex idea of an apple because we are prompted by our experience to suppose that there being an object of a certain nature explains *why* we regularly experience these perceptions together. Our ideas of modes, the third type of mental complex Hume mentions, are our ideas of groups of perceptions for which we don't suppose a single object as the cause. Hume's examples are our ideas of a dance and of beauty. The idea of a dance, for instance, is produced by ideas of movements from various quarters, in various bodies, configured or posed in a variety of ways.

Abstract Ideas

Hume's philosophy of mind is an attempt to account for all the ideas of which the mind is capable. If all ideas come from previous impressions, then how is it that we seem to have general ideas that do not copy any particular experiences? I can talk about the class of dogs, or about sweetness or redness in general, or about the properties of triangles. Yet, I can never experience a dog-in-general; I only experience individual dogs, ones with specific features--pointed or floppy ears, long or short tail, small or large build, curly or straight hair. And so it goes for the other classes: I experience the redness or sweetness of *this* strawberry, the properties of *this* drawing of a scalene triangle. The question which all empiricists must confront is whether we in fact possess "abstract" ideas, even though we experience only particulars; or, whether we use general terms for which there are no ideas to give them meaning.

John Locke proposed that, while all ideas come from experience, we could perform a mental maneuver called "abstraction," by which we use particular ideas to derive abstract ones. His view is that we arrive at abstract ideas by a comparison of concrete complex ideas, noting what they have in common, and then abstracting the commonalties. I may notice, for instance, that my ideas of this strawberry, this rose, and this bird contain the common idea, red, thereby abstracting to the general notion of redness. Abstraction to classes of substances is a little more complicated: After I have determined that this conjunction of qualities is a dog (say, Lassie), and that another conjunction of qualities is also a dog (say, Rover), then I can abstract to the notion of dog-in-general. After I abstract to the notions of dog, monkey, cow, horse, etc., I can eventually abstract to the more general notion of animal, and so forth.

But George Berkeley, another empiricist writing after Locke, disagrees. Since experience is always particular, ideas are always particular, even though we attach them to general terms. When we use these terms, one particular calls to mind other, similar particulars, and this enables us to use these terms to stand for a class of particulars. Hume thinks that Berkeley is right, and he offers to show how his own theory of ideas lends support to Berkeley's view.

One argument Hume offers is that, since ideas are copied from impressions, what is true of the latter must be true of the former. No impression can occur without a determinate (specific) quality and quantity; in other words, impressions are precisely *this* shade of green or *that* degree of hotness, for instance. All ideas then are also determinate. But abstract ideas, were there any, would have to be indeterminate. Therefore, there are no abstract ideas (T 19). Another argument Hume gives begins with an additional empiricist principle of great importance: If experiences are different, they are distinguishable in thought; if they are distinguishable in thought, then they are separable. The converse is also the case: Separability implies distinguishably, and distinguishably implies difference. This follows from the fact that, since we are dealing with the contents of the mind and our objects are mental objects, the boundaries of these objects must be determined by how we are able to think of them. If we can separate them in thought, then they are obviously distinct, and vice-versa. But can we think of a triangle without thinking of its angles? Can we imagine a dog without imagining its ears or tail? Can we think of a line without thinking of its precise length? The answer, Hume contends, is no, and this shows that the idea of a triangle and the idea of its angles, the idea of a dog and the idea of its features, the idea of a line and an idea of its length, are not distinct (T 18-19).

If Hume is right, then Locke is mistaken to hold that we can derive abstract ideas from particular ones by separating off the commonalties from among the various complexes. Is the mental process of abstraction Locke describes plausible? While an empiricist is entitled to think the mind has certain innate capacities, which ones he or she posits depend on the evidence. But what evidence shows whether we can actually think of ideas that are not particular in nature? Since both sides to the dispute admit that we use general terms, that practical bit of evidence

13

doesn't help. From Hume's perspective, Locke's defense of our capacity for abstraction seems weak because Locke begins by theorizing the existence of a mental activity that will get him to the ideas whose existence are in doubt. But Hume consistently wants to consider the nature of our ideas themselves (the only things to which we have immediate access) as the basis for conclusions about what the mind can do.

Further Observations on Hume's Theory of Ideas

It should be clear by now how Hume offers a scientific description of our ordinary mental life. In so doing, he develops a test for the meaningfulness of a term. Words get their meanings from ideas. A word has meaning if and only if the simple component parts of the idea to which the word corresponds are traceable to simple impressions. Why, though, do we need a test, when experience supposedly shows us there can be no ideas that do *not* meet this criterion? Hume's concern is with previous philosophers who have tried to originate theoretical concepts to solve problems, without noticing that these concepts have no source in experience at all. Exactly which concepts are impugned will come to light later. But what is interesting here is that Hume derives a standard by generalization from ordinary experience, which he then sets forth as a test for good philosophy. In so doing, he denies that philosophy can legitimately call upon metaphysical or supernatural concepts--concepts describing something beyond physics and observation, or concepts originating in reason or in rational intuition, or in the mind at birth.

Hume's application of this criterion is the subject of the next few chapters, but it's worth noticing here a certain wrinkle in one of Hume's arguments for his key thesis that all ideas come from previous impressions. Recall Hume's challenge to examine our ideas to see if we can find one *not* traceable to an impression. He thinks we cannot. But what really happens? Every attempt I make to trace an idea to an impression must fail, since every instance of my calling to mind a *preceding* impression is an idea. Impressions occur only in the present and are momentary; of course, they can never be called up in their original force and vivacity. Hence, all of my mental comparisons are necessarily comparisons of one idea to another idea, and I could never verify that an idea is dependent on a precedent impression. Hume never indicates awareness of this problem.

14

Still, why are we inclined to agree so readily that Hume's experiment makes sense? When we run the experiment, we remember having experiences that would have been the source of the ideas, on the assumption that our ideas come from impressions. So it seems that what we prove to ourselves is that our ideas correlate with memories: I know what a lemon tastes like (an idea) and I remember instances of my tasting a lemon (a memory). For any idea I bring to mind, I can find such an experience-memory. Now if Hume shows that there are some special terms referring to notions which can't be traced to experience-memories, he surely has shown something about their status or meaning for us, even if his thesis that all meaningful ideas must be traceable to previous impressions cannot be verified. If we assume about certain ideas that they were acquired from experience, but have no memories of the relevant experiences, something has gone wrong in the way we think about them. So, there is a point to Hume's test, no matter what the problems in his description of it.

Discussion Questions

1. Does it follow from Hume's theory that ideas are actually memories of impressions?
2. Are ideas produced under the influence of drugs a violation of Hume's rule that all meaningful ideas must be traced to preceding impressions?
3. How would Hume explain the source of the idea of God in experience?

Endnotes

1. E.C. Mossner, *The Life of David Hume* (Oxford: Clarendon Press, 1980, 2nd ed.), vii. Unless otherwise stated, the biographic details of Hume related here are based on Mossner's work.
2. Mossner, 51, 64.
3. Hume, "My Own Life," in *Essays: Moral, Political, and Literary*, ed. Eugene Miller (Indianapolis: Liberty Classics, 1985), xxxii-xli.
4. Richard Allenstreet, *The Whole Duty of Man* (London: printed by R. Norton for Robert Pawlet, 1677), two parts in one.

15

5. *The Letters of David Hume*, ed. J.Y.T. Grieg, 2 vols. (Oxford, 1932), Vol. I., 13.
6. Hume, "My Own Life."
7. Paul Wood, "'The Fittest man in the Kingdom': Thomas Reid and the Glasgow Chair of Moral Philosophy," *Hume Studies* XXIII (November 1997): 277-313.
8. Hume, "My Own Life."
9. James Fieser, Introduction to "The Essays on Suicide and the Immortality of the Soul" (1783 edition), *The Writings of David Hume*, ed. James Fieser (Internet Release, 1995).
10. *Letters of David Hume*, Vol. II, 303-306.
11. Mossner, 596.
12. Mossner cites *Private Papers of James Boswell*, 18 vols., ed. Scott and Pottle (New York: 1928-34).
13. Fieser.
14. Among the philosophers Hume mentions are John Locke (*Essay Concerning Human Understanding* [1689]) and Frances Hutcheson (*Essay on the Nature of the Passions and Affections. With Illustrations on the Moral Sense* [1728] and *An Inquiry into the Original of our Ideas of Beauty and Virtue; In Two Treatises* [1725]).
15. Hume's British spelling is "reflexion".
16. After introducing his rule that all ideas are traceable to preceding impressions, Hume notes "one contradictory phenomenon," which shows the rule has one exception. He claims that a person who has experienced every shade of blue, but one, when presented with a gradation of shades absent just that one, will perceive a gap and be able to imagine an idea of the missing shade. Hume's exception has received much discussion, with some questioning whether the observer really has the ability Hume projects. Hume himself is unperturbed, writing, " . . . this instance is so singular, that it is scarcely worth our observing, and does not merit that for it alone we should alter our general maxim" (EHU 21).
17. The seventeenth-century philosophers Descartes and Leibniz are examples of faculty psychologists.
18. Barry Stroud, *Hume* (London: Routledge & Kegan Paul, 1977), 28-29.

2

Causality and Belief

How do we acquire beliefs? After all, to have an idea, to think of something, is not to believe that what one is thinking is in fact the case. We acquire beliefs as the result of enquiries, and Hume divides all "objects of human enquiry" into two types: (1) relations of ideas and (2) matters of fact. Thus, on Hume's theory, our beliefs fall into two corresponding categories, which he examines (EHU 25).

(1) What beliefs are about are their objects. Any belief whose truth is demonstrated by reason has as its object a relation of ideas. An example is, "The sum of the degrees in the angles of a triangle is 180;" this belief has as its object the relation between the idea of a triangle's angles and the idea of 180 degrees. That a belief's truth is demonstrated by reason means it is necessarily true, true under all conditions, because proving it doesn't depend on reference to any circumstances in the world, which are changeable. The truth of a relation of ideas is purely a matter of the mental concepts involved, and once we understand the concepts, we can tell how they are related to each other. Consider other examples: "The sum of four and five is equal to the square root of eight-one," and, "A circle is not a square." We know these statements to be true regardless of whether there are square or circular things, or whether there are objects four or five in number, just by grasping the definitions of the terms involved. Another consequence of the necessity of these truths is that we cannot imagine their contraries--that is, we cannot think of them as false; their falsity is contradictory (EHU 25).

(2) Beliefs about matters of fact, on the other hand, are beliefs for which it is possible to imagine the contrary, since their truth, when they

are true, depends on the way things are. To call a belief a matter-of-fact belief, then, is not to say it is true, but to say that its truth or falsity depends on circumstances. So, for example, it is true in contemporary times that most philosophers are also college professors, but we can easily imagine the opposite--that most philosophers don't teach in colleges, but have other careers along with their writing philosophy. We actually believe this to have been the case in earlier centuries. But what about beliefs concerning nature, where we've never experienced the contrary? For instance, is it a matter of fact, a contingent truth, that the sun will rise tomorrow, or is it a relation of ideas, a necessary truth?

There is no contradiction in the thought that, 24 hours from this current sunrise, the sun does not rise again, even though we think the idea incredible. Just because we've experienced the sunrise every 24 hours doesn't mean we can't think of its being otherwise. On the other hand, that a triangle does not have 180 degrees in the sum of its angles is not just incredible, but also inconceivable. But that bees would make vinegar instead of honey, or that a rock dropped from a cliff would stop in mid-air and sprout a parachute, or that the sun would not rise tomorrow, are all conceivable. These are all matters of fact, and the truths, which contain reference to them, are all contingent (ECU 25-26). The question Hume asks about them is how we come to believe them. They obviously require evidence from experience, but sensations are momentary, and beliefs are enduring. I retain my belief that my coat is in the closet where I hung it, even when I'm not looking in the closet, and I continue to believe that eating dirt will not nourish my body, even though I haven't recently tried it. Hume's science of human nature must explain what prompts us to adopt beliefs whose scope is wider than the experience on which they're based. He argues that only one of the relations yielded by the mind's principles of association can take us beyond present experience--namely causation (T 74).

Causality

All Matters of Fact Based on Cause and Effect

Hume argues for his conclusion that all beliefs in matters of fact are founded on the relation of causality by examining our beliefs:

If you were to ask a man, why he believes any matter of fact, which is absent; for instance, that his friend is in the country, or in

18

France; he would give you a reason; and this reason would be some other fact; as a letter received from him, or the knowledge of his former resolution and promises. A man finding a watch or any other machine in a desert island, would conclude that there had once been men in that island. . . . If we anatomize all the other reasonings of this nature, we shall find that they are based on the relations of cause and effect, . . . (EHU 26-27).

Hume's own examples here pretty obviously support his point: My belief that my friend is in France is due to connecting her presence there to the postmark on her letter. My belief that someone has been on this island is prompted by the causal connection I make between a machine and a designer. But if Hume is right about the general thesis, we should not be able to think of *any* belief in a matter of fact not underpinned by a causal connection. Let's consider some less obvious cases. I believe that dinosaurs lived in pre-historic times. I believe that the moon is not made of green cheese. I believe that the leaves on a sweet gum tree have five points. How is each of *these* beliefs based on a cause-effect connection?

Let's say that my belief that dinosaurs lived in prehistoric times is based on my hearing or reading the results of paleontologists' studies (perhaps second-hand through textbooks in grade school). I assume that the presence of dinosaurs is causally connected to the results of these studies and the conclusions of these researchers, don't I? If someone maintains that her belief about dinosaurs is simply due to believing what someone she trusts tells her, still she must be regarding that person's information ultimately as a causal result of there having been dinosaurs. My belief that the moon is not made of green cheese may be based on evidence about celestial bodies with which I'm familiar. Or perhaps my belief is based on NASA's telling me that none of their astronauts found green cheese on the moon. In any case, I must think of the composition of celestial bodies as the cause of the natural evidence, or I must think of the make-up of the moon as the cause of NASA's or other authorities' conclusions. That the leaves on a gum tree have five points is a belief I've formed by observing the tree outside my window. It's based on the evidence of my senses, but in formulating it, I go beyond the momentary evidence by supposing that there are (enduring) qualities of gum trees that produce (cause) such leaves. Even if I restrict the scope of my belief to *this* gum tree alone, I suppose that the 5-point leaves on this tree endure beyond my perception of them, and so I must assume of *this* tree that it has qualities that cause it to have these leaves.

It does not take consideration of many more examples to vindicate Hume's point that beliefs in matters of fact are based on the relation of cause and effect. The next step in Hume's project, then, is to explore how we know these connections. Beliefs in relations of ideas are known by reason to be necessarily true, but what justifies our beliefs in matters of fact depends on what justifies beliefs in causal connections.

Not by Reason, but by Custom and Habit

Hume argues that the causal beliefs are not produced by reason in the way relations of ideas are. This is proven, first, by the fact that we cannot predict any effect that will occur by merely considering the idea of any particular cause. Examine sugar: Is there anything in the idea we acquire upon a cursory examination that allows us to infer, without further examination, that it is sweet or soluble in water? Our knowledge of the effects of the complex idea we call sugar extends only as far as our experience. If we have only seen its white color and felt its grainy texture, we have no idea of its other effects--how it tastes, whether it dissolves, how it smells. Hume asks us to consider a magnet: Can we infer from our idea of its appearance that it will also attract metal? Can we explain by reason alone why bread nourishes a body or why water suffocates? (EHU 27-28)

Hume anticipates a protest: Were we brought into the world full-grown, but without any experience, surely upon seeing one billiard ball roll, we would be able to predict that it would impart motion to a second upon contact? His response, however, is that we are already conditioned by our experience to believe this, and that without such experience, we could only consider which effects are *conceivable*. But many effects are conceivable--that both balls remain at rest, that the first moves backward in a straight line, that the first ball bounces off the table. Our selection of one over the other, apart from experience, is arbitrary. Hume summarizes his point this way: "In a word, every effect is a distinct event from its cause. It could not, therefore, be discovered in the cause, and the first invention or conception of it, *a priori* [without experience], must be entirely arbitrary" (EHU 30).

Hume might have offered the above summary of his view as a second argument, an argument from the empiricist principle identified in Chapter 1. Recall: If we can think of two things as separable, they must be distinct, and if two things are distinct, we are able to think of them as separable. Whereas Hume presents his original argument that cause and effect associations are not inferred by reason as an empirical one, one supported by looking case by case at our inability to infer particular effects from particular causes, he might have presented a second argument as a conceptual one. Our ability to separate the idea of sugar's whiteness from our idea of its solubility shows, given the principle, that the two are distinct. Since reason can only discern one concept logically contained within another, reason cannot use knowledge of one of sugar's properties (any of the ideas within the complex idea) to infer any of its other properties as a consequence.

Hume has an interesting speculation about the limits of scientific explanation in light of his arguments so far. He writes,

> It is confessed, that the utmost effort of human reason is to reduce the principles, productive of natural phenomena, to a greater simplicity, and to resolve the many particular effects into a few general causes, ... But as to the causes of these general causes, we should in vain attempt their discovery; nor shall we ever be able to satisfy ourselves, by any particular explication of them. These ultimate springs and principles are shut up from human curiosity and enquiry. Elasticity, gravity, cohesion of parts, communication of motion by impulse; these are probably the ultimate causes and principles which we shall ever discover in nature; . . .(EHU 30).

Hume's observation is interesting for two reasons. One is that it exemplifies his mindfulness of the new science, as embodied in the theories of Newton, who formulated the law of gravity and the laws of physical motion, and Boyle[1], author of the modern corpuscular theory of physics. In Boyle's view, the causal properties of objects in the world are due to the features of their minute constituent parts, or corpuscles, or atoms. On this theory, which figures even more prominently in Locke's work on perception, the particles which make up natural objects in the world have a certain figure, number, motion, mass, and texture; these features determine the object's nature and its effects on objects of different natural kinds, which interact with each other by contact or impulse. So, for instance, the corpuscular composition of fire and of wax determines that the one melts and vaporizes the other.

The second reason Hume's observation is noteworthy is that it seems to imply that scientific explanations stop at the principles of motion of the observable physical objects because we cannot go deeper in our enquiries to the "ultimate springs and principles" of the unseen, tiny parts. And this makes it sound as though the problem lies with something contingent--namely, with facts about our investigatory

21

abilities and our limited senses, such that if we overcame these limitations, we might know the necessary connection of causality. In other words, it sounds as though we might know objective causal connections if we only had more powerful microscopes.

But such an implication is inconsistent with Hume's own arguments. For his own arguments imply that our inability to infer effects from the mere idea of an object or of a kind of object is not a contingent limitation, but one due to the way we must think about objects, which he has identified with complex ideas. If it's given that complex ideas can be broken into simples, then all complexes are made of intellectually separable parts; this means that all simple qualities are separate. Consider: The bright orange light we identify as a fire is accompanied by heat; consequently, we add heat to the complex idea, but our only ground for doing so is experiencing heat in conjunction with the other sensations. We have no mental ground on which to unite cause and effect without experience. The qualities of even the minute parts, were we to perceive them, are in the same boat, and so we just push the problem to a different level if we try to find our causal explanations there. (It's as though we are dealing with tiny billiard balls, instead of with large ones.) So, science can never solve the problem of our trying to know effects we have not experienced.

So how do we *ever* arrive at beliefs concerning causes and effects, which are supposed to take us beyond present experience, when such beliefs have to be based on present experience? If I can add to my present experience and my memory of past experience a belief that the future will be like the past, then I could formulate an argument with a conclusion about the future. It would go like this: (1) In the past, my experience of fire has been conjoined with the experience of heat; (2) The future will resemble the past; (3) Therefore, my experiences of fire and heat will be conjoined in the future. The conclusion gets us to the future, as causal connections should; so it is indicative for us of causality. But, as Hume points out, the second premise is itself based on experience, namely, on experience of past pasts and past futures, and so its justification is circular: (1) In the past, future experiences have resembled past experiences; (2) The future will resemble the past; (3) Therefore, in the future, future experiences will resemble past experiences. The conclusion and the second premise are the same; this attempt to justify conclusions about the future goes no place fast.

Hume focuses instead on a non-rational principle of human nature that gets us beyond present experience: namely, custom and habit. The reason why a person with no experience, brought full-grown into the world, has no grounds on which to predict how one rolling billiard ball

22

will affect another is that she has no basis for forming a habit of association between the one event and any other. Custom and habit allow the human mind to forge a mental connection between ideas that have no conceptual connection. If, in one instance after another, I see the second ball roll forward on impact with the first, I develop a habit of associating the first movement with the second. The habit becomes reinforced to the point that my mind passes from the experience of the first event to an expectation of the second, even before it happens. And so for other events we term causes and effects: I believe the sun will rise tomorrow because I'm conditioned by past experience to expect it. I believe that paper burns and fiberglass doesn't because I have a repeated conjunction of the experience of fire with the experience of burning paper, and a different constant conjunction of the perception of fire and the perception of non-ignited fiberglass. My mind moves beyond the moment to the future, not because reason finds the connection between ideas, but because custom creates it:

> Custom, then, is the great guide of human life. It is a principle alone which renders our experience useful to us, and makes us expect, for the future, a similar train of events with those which have appeared in the past. Without the influence of custom we should be entirely ignorant of every matter of fact beyond what is immediately present to the memory and senses. We should never know how to adjust means to ends, or to employ our natural powers in the production of any effect. There would be an end at once of all action, as well as of the chief part of speculation (EHU 44-45).

The Idea of Necessary Connection

Any plausible account of how we make causal connections must distinguish between mere correlation and causation. In the past, the tobacco industry was fond of reminding consumers of the difference between the two when it came to smoking and lung cancer. But we are now all convinced the connection between smoking and lung cancer is causal. What does this mean, on Hume's analysis, when compared to correlation? Hume finds in our idea of causality three component ideas.

The first is *contiguity*: The two experiences come to me constantly conjoined, contiguously, in time and space. Perceptions separated in time and space give us no grounds for correlation; hence, causation at a distance is impossible. This is not to rule out, however, a chain of causal connections joining an initial cause to a last one, non-contiguous with the first. The second component of causation is *succession*, with cause preceding effect. Hume argues that if an effect could occur at the same time as its cause, then *all* events would occur at the same time. This is because we suppose all events have a cause, which leads necessarily to the conclusion that all events are causally connected. Thus, as soon as one event in the universe occurs, all must. Since this is absurd, we regard causes and effects as in succession (T 75-76).

Contiguity and succession give us correlation, but when we think of causality, we think of the cause *producing* the effect. In other words, we think that the cause *necessitates* the effect, which is a way of saying that when the first occurs, it's not just that the second *does* occur, but that it *must*. The third and crucial element in our idea of causality is the idea of *necessary connection*. From our viewpoint, the necessity is captured in our believing that the cause and effect will always occur together. If fire causes heat, then every time we have fire, we will have heat. If gum trees produce five-pointed leaves in the spring, then every time we have a gum tree in the spring, we will have five-pointed leaves. Of course, when we say that smoking causes lung cancer, we don't mean that every time we have an instance of even chronic smoking, we will find lung cancer. But the correlation is strong enough to lead us to explain the inconstancies by the supposition that we haven't perceived the entire cause. We speculate that when other conditions obtain, conditions that we are unable yet in our research on cancer to articulate, then those, along with smoking, will always be found with lung cancer.

So Hume asks: From where do we get the idea of necessary connection that binds the cause to the effect? The idea must come from experience, on his view--traceable to either an impression of sensation or an impression of reflection. But when we examine our outward experience, Hume argues, we find only one impression (or set of impressions) followed by another, but no impression of the connection between them: the motion of one billiard ball and the motion of a second billiard ball, the light of the fire and then the heat, the bare tree and then its leaves. We see in fact that one follows the other, but we find no impression of the power one has to produce the other, no impression of the necessity that cements the two events together.

Might the idea of necessity be derived, alternatively, from an inward experience, that is, one produced by reflection on what happens when we cause our own actions to occur? After all, we must be most intimately acquainted with the experience of causing our bodies to move in various ways; we ought to be able to find a perception of the

24

connection between cause and effect there. Locke argues that this is where we find the source of the idea of power. But Hume disagrees. Action involves bodily movement, and Hume argues that to understand how we initiate action requires an understanding of how the mind, where the impulse to action originates, causes a change in the body. I desire or "will" my leg to move, and my leg moves: How? Do I really experience the connection between the two? This connection is one of the biggest mysteries in philosophy, and so not a promising source, Hume thinks, for the idea of necessity.

There is no impression for the idea of necessity. Rather, Hume describes the psychological process that produces belief in causal connections this way: The constant conjunction of perceived events produces in us an association of the two perceptions, until the association becomes so strong that we feel a "determination of the mind" to pass from the perception of the first to a thought of the second (an effect of custom and habit). When we reach this point, we posit a necessary connection between the events. Our mind fills in the gaps in our experience by supplying the notion that the two events are necessarily bound to each other, even though they are experienced distinctly. Since Hume has argued that we have no ideas not derived from experience, and since terms get their meaning from their corresponding ideas, here he has unearthed a term, namely, necessary connection, that does not pass the test for meaningfulness.

One might suggest that the feeling of determination of the mind to move to a future idea, this sentiment of expectation of one event upon another, *is* the impression to which we can trace the idea of necessary connection. This is precisely Hume's point:

> Upon the whole, necessity is something, that exists in the mind, not in objects; nor is it possible for us ever to form the most distant idea of it , consider'd as a quality in bodies. Either we have no idea of necessity, or necessity is nothing but that determination of the thought to pass from causes to effects and from effects to causes, according to their experience'd union (T 165-66).

There is no idea of necessity in the sense that scientists and philosophers have thought of it, as binding effects to their causes. There is only an idea of a mental anticipation of effect upon cause. Hume puts the same point in the *Enquiry* this way:

> This connexion, therefore, which we feel in the mind, this customary transition of the imagination from one object to its usual

attendant, is the sentiment or impression from which we form the idea of power or necessary connexion. Nothing farther is in the case (EHU 75).

Hume's conclusion is that what we take for the notion of necessity is really descriptive of our own minds and of our own expectations. As some authors have described it, when we think causality is found outside of us, it is because we project onto the world, and think we have discovered there, what we actually find inside ourselves.[2]

Belief

What is a Belief?

Thinking of snow in Africa and believing it is snowing in Africa are two different things, even though both are complex ideas with the same contents. When someone tells me an incredible story, in order to understand it, I have to form the same ideas the other person has, but I may not believe the story. The difference between my belief and disbelief does not lie in any idea added to the one that the other lacks, but rather, in my attitude toward the story. Since what the imagined idea represents and what the believed idea represents are the same, the only way a belief can be distinguished from an idea I entertain is by a phenomenal, or feeling, dimension. In the *Enquiry*, Hume says:

> It follows, therefore, that the difference between *fiction* and *belief* lies in some sentiment or feeling, which is annexed to the latter, not to the former, and which depends not on the will, nor can be commanded at pleasure. It must be excited by nature, like all other sentiments; and must arise from the particular situation in which the mind is placed at any juncture (EHU 48).

The sentiment which attaches to an idea when we are overcome with belief is indefinable; like other impressions and feelings--coldness or anger, etc.-- it is an original feeling, not reducible to any other. It is, Hume says, the sentiment of belief. But in the *Treatise of Human Nature*, Hume defines a belief as "A LIVELY IDEA RELATED TO OR ASSOCIATED WITH A PRESENT IMPRESSION" (T 96). This description looks little like the one from the *Enquiry*, which defines belief in terms of sentiment. Do they mean the same thing?

26

We know that a belief is a complex idea formed as a result of a mental habit of associating experiences. But Hume also insists that the relation to a present impression is part of the definition of belief because beliefs are triggered by experiences or impressions after the mental habit is acquired. What he has in mind is this: A person who walks to the edge of a deep river stops immediately; she needs no further experience to know that if she takes another step, she will fall into the water and drown. The current impressions trigger her belief that walking into deep water causes one to drown, although the belief itself is actually the product of causal associations already well-entrenched. When I look out the window to see what sort of day it is, and I find it pouring rain, I don't need further information to conclude that I will get wet if I go out without an umbrella or a raincoat. The sight of the rain is a catalyst to my belief, but only because I am primed or disposed by prior experience to have the belief. So, when Hume defines a belief as a lively idea associated with a present impression, he has in mind that, even though all beliefs depend on prior conditioning, they come to mind spontaneously in ordinary life, when triggered by current experience. The custom, he says, operates in practical situations before we have time to reflect (T 101-104).

The liveliness of the idea we call belief is the other important feature of Hume's definition from the *Treatise*, since he makes the point there, as well as in the *Enquiry*, that belief can only be distinguished from non-belief by its feeling. The present impression is also crucial in this feature of belief, since Hume explains that it is the present impression associated with an idea that boosts the vivacity of that idea to the intensity of belief (T 98-106). Hume argues that experiences always give a lift to their associated ideas. Consider the relation of contiguity that might hold between an impression and an idea. I have all sorts of ideas, vague much of the time, of my hometown, located a continent away from where I now reside. When I get on a plane headed for that town, as I progress on the trip and look out the window of the plane, the ideas of the town I am soon to visit acquire a vivacity and detail that they typically lack in my life away. The experience of locations contiguous to my hometown somehow boosts the forcefulness of my ideas of the town as I reminisce.

Now take the relation of causality. My past experience has produced in me an association of cherry trees with white blossoms. I'm on a walk in the springtime, and I see a tree in the distance arrayed in white blossoms. The vivacity of my impression gets transferred to the associated idea, the cherry tree. The idea that this tree with white blossoms is a cherry tree, or that cherry trees have white blossoms, is

27

lifted in vivacity to the status of belief. I still might entertain the idea that cherry blossoms are violet, perhaps writing a science fiction tale about a world where nature behaves differently from nature in our world; but this fictional idea is less lively than my idea that cherry blossoms are white. The former is an idea of the imagination, and the latter, one of belief. Similarly, as I look out the window at the pouring rain, my present impressions boost the vividness of my idea that rain makes people and things wet, and I believe at this moment that I will get wet if I go out without cover. Such is how beliefs are the most vivacious ideas we experience, and only pale in comparison to impressions, from which they derive their vivacity.

Returning, then, to the simpler description of belief from the *Enquiry*, belief as a sentiment "annexed" to an idea: Is it consistent with the *Treatise* account, even though it lacks the detail of the other? I think there is a problem with reconciling the two definitions. Simply adding a "sentiment of belief" (something like a feeling of conviction) to a complex of ideas is not identical to having those ideas take on a certain force and vivacity, in the way the *Treatise* account indicates the ideas of belief do. The *Enquiry* implies that the sentiment of belief could be separated from the complex idea as all simples in a complex can be. But since all ideas have some degree of force and vivacity, it must be impossible to separate the having of an idea from the sentiment with which it is felt. In other words, to have an idea at all, whether it is of memory, imagination, or belief, is to experience it with some degree of liveliness. The *Treatise* definition seems preferable, then, to the *Enquiry* account of belief, since it is consistent with inseparability of the phenomenal dimension of belief from the cognitive (that is, content) dimension of belief. Hume offers some further reflections on the nature of belief in his Appendix to the *Treatise* (623-27), which have led some readers to think he was dissatisfied with his account; but his discussion there is opaque and open to various interpretations.

Beliefs Are Practical

Hume's description of belief raises an interesting question: Do I only believe ideas brought before the mind by present experiences and manifested in behavior? Or do I also believe ideas of which I was once aware, but happen not to be connected with any behavior of mine just now? For instance, do I believe that George Washington was the first President of the United States when I'm thinking about how to get the stains out of my socks? I think the right reply is that I am disposed to believe it, and if a present impression were supplied to trigger the belief, then I do believe it. For example, if someone asked whether I believed that George Washington was the first President of the United States, my answer is "yes," and my answer is right, since I have a lively idea associated with a present impression. We might say that memories are ideas that we are disposed to believe. Under the proper conditions they are aroused by a stimulus and play a practical part in life. This perspective has led some readers to think that Hume's view is that belief is nothing but the behavior that manifests it. Such a position is called "behaviorism." But given Hume's detailed treatment of belief as an idea, I see little ground for accepting this interpretation, which denies that belief is a mental state, and indeed denies the existence of all mental states, explaining our mental life instead in terms of actions.

So, while Hume is not a behaviorist, he is interested in the fact that beliefs are uniquely situated among all our ideas to influence actions. This is consistent with his announced intent on the title page of the *Treatise* that his study is "an attempt to introduce the experimental method of reasoning into moral subjects"--that is, to do a scientific treatment of humans as practical beings. Hume observes that it is fortunate for us that imagined ideas cannot play the role in motivation that beliefs can, or we would be moved in all sorts of fruitless and arbitrary directions. Readers debate exactly what role in motivation beliefs play, in light of views Hume expresses in his psychology of the passions, which is here discussed in Chapter 4.

It is safe to say here, however, that beliefs give us practical information by which we guide our behavior in view of what we want, and they arouse passions or feelings in light of our own emotional dispositions. If I am a risk-averse person, the belief that mountain climbing is fraught with danger will arouse in me a passion of fear that will likely deter me from making mountain climbing my avocation. Of course, imagining these dangers might have the same effect, but this is only because I believe them to be likely. If I thought they were merely imaginary, I wouldn't respond by feeling real fear at their thought. Conversely, our emotional dispositions are, Hume says, conducive to certain beliefs: An unconfident person more easily believes that her project has severe flaws than a confident person believes the same about hers (T 119-120). Belief and imagination are also mutually influential: Belief conduces to a lively imagination, and a lively imagination promotes belief. An eloquent and colorful storyteller can sometimes provoke our assent with a forcefulness that even overcomes the effect of custom, and persuade us to believe something contrary to our ordinary experience (T 123).

29

Empiricism and Skepticism

Rationalism and Empiricism

With Hume's discussion of causality and belief in place, it is now easier to articulate the difference between rationalism and empiricism. The dispute between rationalists and empiricists is basically over whether reason ultimately justifies belief or whether experience does. In this debate, it is important to remember that reason is understood as the discernment of logical relations between ideas or between thoughts. Philosophers think of reason in this sense as a combination of intuition, an immediate grasp of truths, and demonstration, logical deductions constructed from these truths. Rationalists are characterized by two connected theses: (1) that the mind has innate ideas and (2) that beliefs about the world can be justified by reason. If reason is to justify belief on its own, there must be some contents in the mind with which it can work before it has experience. Thus, a defense of innate ideas is a rationalist mark. Empiricists, on the other hand, deny both (1) and (2).

It looks as though the focus of the rationalist-empiricist dispute is over how ideas and beliefs are acquired. This issue does play a part in the debate, but only because acquisition is related to justification. To justify is to give good reasons why, and anything that hails from reason itself is already necessarily supported by reasons. If I can deduce that the sun will rise tomorrow, then I would be irrational not to believe it. So, if the rationalist can show (a) that beliefs about the world are produced by reason, then those beliefs must be justified. The other way the rationalist can go is to claim (b) that beliefs about the world come from the senses, but that reason guarantees for us that sense perception is reliable. Leibniz is a case of (a), and Descartes of (b).

Descartes agrees we have many beliefs based on sense experience, but he thinks experience is not itself justifying. That we see something, for instance, is not necessarily a good reason to think it's just the way we see it. So, Descartes attempts to use reason to justify sense perception as a source of beliefs. He does this, first, by using his innate idea of God, along with other principles, to demonstrate God's existence. Then he argues that, since God is by definition good and perfect, the faculty of sense perception, which God gave us, is also error-free. It follows that *when* we use sense perception properly (and we don't always), we can't be mistaken in the beliefs it produces. Leibniz, on the other hand, argues that each causal belief about the world can actually be produced by reason, if we only have complete

30

knowledge of the concepts our beliefs are about. In other words, he thinks we can deduce from some of the properties of sugar how it will interact with other substances, even before we have experience of the results. He thinks that having the concept involves understanding the essence of the substance and that all its properties follow logically from its essence. So, I don't need experience to conclude that water will suffocate or that fire is hot. I need only have a complete grasp of their essences. But Hume, of course, thinks such deductions are impossible.

Skepticism and Naturalism

There are different ways of being a skeptic, but skepticism is commonly defined as the view that we have no knowledge of the world outside the mind. It is considered a negative position, rather than a constructive one, since the skeptical position is forced upon one whose thinking leads to the conclusion that there are no materials out of which to construct a positive theory of knowledge. Given Hume's argument that we can never find an impression of necessary connection beyond the feeling of determination of the mind, he has claim to the title "the great skeptic." Among the significant implications of his analysis, which is widely adopted among empirically-minded philosophers, are: Inductive reasoning, the process of drawing general conclusions from individual experiences, is never conclusive; and the laws of nature are not necessary in the sense that we are tempted to think they are.

Naturalists in philosophy offer constructive accounts of the phenomena they study in terms of qualities to which the senses have access in the natural world, that is, without reference to supernatural or metaphysical properties inaccessible by the ordinary senses. One cannot be both a naturalist and a skeptic about the same phenomena, and insofar as Hume gives a positive account of belief-formation and causal "reasoning" in the way he does, he appears to be a naturalist. It is important to note that our process of forming causal beliefs is often called "causal reasoning," or "matter-of-fact" reasoning even though Hume has made it clear that this is not the work of reason in the formal sense (demonstrative reason). But arriving at beliefs is an inferential process, that is, a mental movement from one perception to another; thus, calling this movement of thought "reasoning" is apt, even though it depends crucially on custom and habit, a non-rational principle.

Hume takes the further anti-skeptical step in the *Treatise* of deriving eight norms for proper causal reasoning from his observations

31

of human nature (T 173-76). If causality is not something in the external world, but something inside of us, how can anyone get it wrong? But of course, we get it wrong, and Hume's discussion on the influence of the passions and of the imagination on belief explains in part how and why we sometimes get it wrong. Some years ago, two scientists at the University of Utah announced that they had discovered the process of cold fusion, but later it was revealed they had mistaken their results. This was not a hoax on their part, but a genuine, honest leap to a conclusion that later proved unjustified by the consistent observations. Sometimes when we want badly to believe something, our mind feels the determination that ordinarily constitutes a causal connection before the normal conditions for causal connections obtain.

Hume is keenly aware of these aspects of human nature too and accounts for them by the principles he has discovered in ordinary human mental life. Imagination and passion are ordinary parts of the human constitution; sometimes they influence belief in misleading ways and sometimes not. It's clear that Hume's conclusions concerning causality are not entirely skeptical, and his naturalistic derivation of norms for human life is constructive and practical. This approach later takes on a primary importance in his moral philosophy.

Discussion Questions

1. Explain how the belief that Loch Ness is in Scotland is based on a relation of cause and effect.
2. Can my idea that two plus five equals seven (a relation of ideas) be a belief, according to Hume's definition of belief as "a lively idea associated with a present impression"?
3. Give some examples of mistaken causal reasoning.

Endnotes

1. Robert Boyle, *The Works of the Honorable Robert Boyle*, ed. Thomas Birch, 6 vols., London, 1672.
2. This is called "the projectivist" view of necessity: We project onto the world what we find inside of ourselves. Simon Blackburn attributes this view to Hume in *Spreading the Word* (Oxford: Clarendon Press, 1980), 210-11.

3
Belief in the Physical World and the Self

Why Do We Believe in the Existence of Objects?

All of our beliefs in matters of fact, on Hume's theory, are based on a habit of associating one experience with another, until we come to believe that the one is the cause of the other. But if we take such beliefs to be about objects in the world, and not merely about our perceptions, our beliefs presuppose yet other beliefs--namely beliefs in the existence of objects. The beliefs Hume has so far analyzed represent to us the way things are arranged, for instance: "The tea kettle is on the stove," "Wax melts in the heat," or "The sun will rise tomorrow." We don't think we're talking only about our mental states when we say these things; but how do we come to believe in the existence of these objects? In coming to believe, say, that the sun exists, it is not the case that we can correlate our experiences of the sun with the sun itself; we can only connect experiences with other experiences--some perceptions of the sun with other perceptions of the sun. So, when we say that the sun causes us to feel hot, we're connecting our perceptions of brightness, light, etc., which constitute our complex idea of the sun, with our perception of heat. Believing the sun exists is another thing.

So far, then, we have an account of how we attribute qualities to objects; but we have no account of how we come to believe that objects exist outside the mind. Hume himself points out that to believe an object exists is not to attribute a new property to it (T 94). My idea of Santa Claus has no different content whether I believe he exists or not;

33

but Hume thinks that the idea of an existent Santa is thought or experienced in a different, more vivacious way. In whatever way we come to the belief in the existence of objects, then, it requires a different psychological process from the one described as underlying matter-of-fact beliefs. And the issue involves another vexing question: How do I arrive at the idea of myself, or of my mind, as the subject, or possessor, of these perceptions, when all the perceptions in my mind, on which my ideas must be based, are presumably of other objects?

Hume's next inquiry, then, is: What causes lead us to believe in the existence of "bodies"? ("Body" is a term used for all physical objects, not just organisms.) It's futile, Hume says, to ask whether there are bodies or not; we can't answer this question, and so we simply take it for granted. Given that our perceptions are the ground for any of our beliefs, his question gets divided into two related issues: (1) Why we presume bodies to have a *continued* existence, even when we are not perceiving them, and (2) why we presume bodies to have a *distinct* existence, that is, an existence external to the mind and apart from our perceptions (T 188). In his discussion of this topic, Hume separates ordinary thought from the thought of philosophers. He is interested in showing how people naturally come to believe in external objects, but he is also interested in showing how what past philosophers have said on the topic is mistaken. Ordinary people (sometimes called, "the vulgar," not a derogatory term at the time) mistake their perceptions to be objects; they think the external objects are actually contained in their experience. But this thought is confused, since experience is mental, and objects are supposed to be physical. Philosophers, on the other hand, recognize that our perceptions are purely mental, and then they theorize that there is also a world of physical substance, which causes the perceptions, but which itself is unknowable, since it is always beyond experience. Hume calls the belief that there exist both objects and perceptions of objects a belief in "double existence." He thinks this belief is worse off than the views of the vulgar. We shall later see why.

Idea of Objects Not Gotten by the Senses or Reason

It seems obvious to us that we get the idea of external objects directly from the senses: We just see them, feel them, taste them, hear them. I simply perceive my arm or my hand as outside of my mind, and the book as beyond my hand, and the table as beyond the book; as I look out the window, I seem to perceive a house as being in the distance, and a tree beyond it, and so on (T 190-91). But my perception of "outness," so to speak, cannot be the work of the senses alone, Hume argues, for three reasons. (1) We perceive impressions, not objects. Of course, what he means is that our experiences or perceptions *are* impressions. Even if we take them to be experiences *of* objects, what we have immediate and direct access to are just the experiences or impressions in the mind, and nothing outside of them. (2) Also, our idea of the externality of objects cannot come from the senses alone because we agree that it makes no sense to think of impressions like sounds, tastes, and smells, as existing in things outside the mind. While I might call the grapefruit "sour", I don't mean the grapefruit is experiencing a sour taste; I attribute the sour taste only to myself, the perceiver. So, all of our perceptions are internal and give us no idea of externality. (3) Further, in cases where we *do* take our perceptions to be experiences of something outside of us, as in our feeling a bulk and attributing it to the grapefruit itself, the senses do not give us this notion of "outness" immediately. The mind performs a kind of inference, a line of thinking, to arrive at the idea of the external object. This means that the senses cannot on their own give us the idea of an independent, or *distinct*, world (T 191).

Neither can the senses alone be the source of the idea of *continued* existence. Only a small number of the objects we believe to exist are present to the senses at any given time. When I close my eyes, or merely blink, these letters and the paper on which they are printed disappear from my senses; when I leave the room, the desk, chair, lamp, and books are no longer present to my senses. But I still think of these objects as continuing to exist when I don't perceive them; I don't regard them as popping in and out of existence as they do or don't come under the scrutiny of my senses. If the senses alone were the origin of the idea of continued existence, Hume argues, they would have to perceive what they can't perceive--objects that are not present to them. Hume's conclusion is that the notion of a continued and distinct existence never arises from experience (T 191-92).

So, is it reason that leads us to believe in the independent and continued existence of objects? (Since a belief is a lively idea, the switch from the question of the origin of the idea to the origin of the belief is only a minor one; if reason leads to the belief that there are objects, it might also be the source of the idea of objects.) Since philosophers deal in reasoned argumentation, Hume notes that they conclude that everything appearing to the mind is a perception, and thus, intermittent and dependent on the mind for its existence. But ordinary people pay no attention to these arguments; rather, they "confound perceptions and objects, and attribute a distinct continu'd existence to the very things they feel or see" (T 193). Their belief that they perceive objects directly is not a product of rational reflection.

Remember, deductive reason deals with relations of ideas, and causal "reasoning" (which is essentially custom or habit) deals with matters of fact. Since a relation of ideas is about just that--our ideas, and not about objects--deductive reason can't be the source of the belief in an object's existence. The only other option then is that belief in objects is the conclusion of causal reasoning. But if ordinary people do not distinguish their perceptions from the objects in the first place, they could never *infer*, or reason to, the existence of the latter from the former. Nor could they reason to a conclusion about the causes of their perceptions, since causal reasoning requires correlation of experiences. If we don't typically distinguish between experiences and objects, we have no basis for a correlation between them. And even if we did typically make such a distinction, as some more reflective people do, we still could not make a causal connection between them, given that we only have access to objects through our perceptions and can only correlate perceptions with other perceptions. It's impossible to conclude through *any* line of reasoning that objects cause perceptions (T 193).

It's not surprising that Hume argues that the idea of physical objects doesn't hail from reason. However, how is it that we all believe in the existence of such objects when the idea doesn't come from experience either?!

Coherence and Constancy and the Imagination

Hume maintains that it must be the imagination that gives rise to the notion of continued and distinct existence. How? For one thing, all impressions are internal and intermittent; from moment to moment what I feel in my experience differs--changing colors, changing sounds, changing feelings. But, as we have noted, it is only some of these that we believe to be distinct from us and continuing. We don't, for instance, believe our feelings of love and hatred or our tastes of sweetness or bitterness to be something outside of ourselves. Is there some quality of perceptions that prompts us to attribute a continued and distinct existence to some and not to others? It can be neither the involuntariness nor the force and vivacity of some impressions as opposed to others. Passions and affections are among the most forceful, but are as involuntary as the ideas of shape and extension; yet, we

36

suppose the former to be mind-dependent and fleeting, but the latter to be enduring qualities of physical objects (T 194).

We find that those impressions to which we attribute a continued existence have a constancy, which distinguishes them from the impressions whose existence we regard as mind-dependent. The mountains, houses, and trees, which are presently in my sight, have always appeared to me in a certain arrangement. When I lose sight of them by shutting my eyes or turning my head, they later return without any change in their configuration. Such constancy does admit of exceptions: Objects often change their position and qualities after a short interruption, or even become unrecognizable. The tree loses its leaves; the house loses a shutter or gets a new color; the mountain acquires a white cap. However, the changes exhibit a kind of coherence and regularity, which is the foundation of a kind of reasoning, and, Hume says, produces the opinion of continued existence (T 194-97). For example, when I return to my living room after an hour, the fire in my fireplace is not the same as I left it, but I'm accustomed to seeing a similar alteration in a similar time. When I return in autumn to a park I visited in the summer, it looks very different. The leaves on the trees have changed color, and some trees are partly bare; the grass has yellowed, and the sidewalks are strewn with debris. But I recognize it as the same park because it changes periodically and systematically.

The inference to external objects involves custom and experience, as does our reasoning concerning causes and effects, but the two are really very different. Hume says the former type of argument relies on custom in an indirect manner. This is because when we infer the continued existence of objects, it is in order to project a greater regularity than what is observed in perception. Any degree of regularity in our perceptions cannot be the basis for inferring a greater degree of regularity in the objects, which are not perceived, since this inference supposes a habit acquired by what was never present to the mind. Constant repetition, the key to causal associations, cannot get us beyond the experiences themselves. So, the extending of custom and reason beyond the perceptions to external objects must arise from the work of other principles--namely, coherence and constancy (T 197-98).

Neither coherence nor constancy of experiences alone is sufficient to explain our existence beliefs fully; rather, Hume says, both are necessary. Each gets us to think of a continued existence--that is, of objects existing even though we don't perceive them. Continued existence prompts us, then, to think of distinct existence, since objects existing when I don't perceive them must be distinct from me. Consider *coherence* first. My perceptions have a kind of coherence, which I

37

extend by supposing the continued existence of objects. I live on the second floor of my apartment building. Someone knocks at the door. I assume that person climbed the stairs--which I don't see at present--since everything in my past experience makes me believe that people don't float up or fly. I suppose the hallway and its floor exist and the person at my door is standing on it. Or if I get a letter from a friend in a distant country, I believe my friend still exists and I suppose a plane I did not perceive transported the letter. When I hear the noise of a door opening in the other room, I suppose the door exists even though I don't have any other perceptual evidence of it at this moment. I'm accustomed to a constant conjunction of a creak with the experience of a door moving on hinges, which I call upon here, even though I do not in this particular instance perceive both of the events. My previous causal associations run contrary to present belief, unless I suppose that the door still remains, and that it was opened without my perceiving it. My world of beliefs is fraught with contradiction unless I suppose the continued existence of objects: "And this observation, which was at first entirely arbitrary and hypothetical, acquires a force and evidence by its being the only one, upon which I can reconcile these contradictions" (T 196-97). "Here then I am naturally led to regard the world, as something real and durable, and as preserving its existence, even when it is no longer present to my perception" (T 197).

The imagination is at work in this kind of belief formation because the imagination has a tendency to follow a train of thinking once started, even when present experience doesn't bear it up. Our perceptions have a coherence that is magnified when we suppose objects to have a continued existence. This continuing object is a fiction of the imagination, by which the unchanging object is supposed to participate in the changes of our perceptions (T200-201). But coherence alone won't get us to distinct existence of the entire world; as we have seen, that also requires the principle of constancy.

Now consider *constancy*. There are all sorts of objects, remote from me, which appear, disappear, and then re-appear with a sort of consistency. The constant reappearance of resembling perceptions makes for an easy transition of the mind along the ideas of the interrupted perceptions, and this feeling is almost the same as that of one constant and uninterrupted perception (T 204). For instance, my perception of the moon or the ocean comes and goes; if I were to regard these objects as destroyed when I am not perceiving them, and then newly created each time I perceive them again, I would run into a psychological conflict. Hume says that we disguise the interruption in our perceptions by supposing a fiction of continued existence (205-06).

Our conception of the object acquires a force and vivacity from the resemblance of the broken impressions to one another, and this relation renders a belief in the existence of the object. But, Hume notes, there is a confusion in ordinary thinking: People take their perceptions to be their only objects and suppose material existence is present to the mind.

The Philosophers' Quandary

A summary of Hume's account of how ordinary people arrive at the belief in the continued and independent existence of objects is the following. People suppose their perceptions to be the objects and yet believe in the continued existence of matter. But upon the supposition that perceptions are their objects, it is simply false that objects are continuing through the interruptions. But because the perceptions bear such a strong resemblance to one another, the imagination is prompted into originating the fiction of a continued existence to remedy a contradiction; this is the contradiction between the propensity to think objects continue during interruptions and the implication of supposing that perceptions are our objects--that objects are interrupted. This fiction becomes a belief when it is boosted in force and vivacity by remembered impressions.

Philosophers realize the fallacy in the position of the typical person. Simple experiments show that perceptions have no external existence: They vary with our positions; objects look smaller or larger depending on where the perceiver is situated. Likewise, tastes, colors, and so forth vary with the situation and condition of the perceiver. All of this evidence militates against the conclusion that our perceptions are external objects. Philosophers change their systems in light of the conclusion that perceptions have no external existence, and they distinguish between the perceptions and the objects, adopting the belief in double existence. But, Hume argues, (1) their view depends on the views of the vulgar, plus (2) it has some problems peculiar to it.

(1) As he says, if philosophers were not first persuaded of the ordinary view, they would never come to the belief in double existence. Consider: Ordinary folk suppose the continued existence of their objects, which are perceptions; philosophers see that perceptions are dependent. Philosophers ought to conclude, then, that objects have no continuous existence. Instead, they propose to separate perceptions from objects (T 214-215). They ascribe contrary qualities to different things: Interruption to the perceptions, and continuance to objects. They

are led this way because they will not relinquish the view of the vulgar that objects of perception are continuous.

(2) On top of this, the doctrine of double existence is problematic on its own: There is no way to explain how anyone would ever believe it. Hume argues that it would never be recommended to (causal) reason, or to the imagination. As we know, causal reasoning can only make correlations between perceptions, and never between objects and perceptions, so we cannot make an inference to the existence of objects that way. As for imagination, Hume thinks there is no plausible explanation why, given the supposition that our perceptions are broken and interrupted, we would imagine *another* existence, resembling these perceptions, but continued and uninterrupted. The only thing to recommend the philosophers' view is the view of the vulgar, upon which the former depends (T 213-15)

How Do We Get the Idea of the Self?

Hume's confrontation with the problem of the external world leads to a related question: How do I acquire an idea of the self, the possessor, or subject, of the experiences? Some philosophers have maintained that we are always aware of ourselves, but when I look inward for a perception of the self, all I find are changing impressions and ideas. Where do I get a notion of the mind in which all these perceptions are passing? Since the empiricist rule says that all genuine ideas are traceable to previous impressions, if I have an understandable idea of the self, there must be an impression, or a set of impressions, from which the idea is derived. Our perceptions are constantly in flux, but the self is that thing which remains constant through all the changes in our perceptions. So, if we are to have an impression from which the idea of self is derived, it must be an experience continuing throughout all the other changes of experience.

Hard as we search, we can find no constant perception inside ourselves. Hume compares the mind to a theater:

> The mind is a kind of theatre, where several perceptions successively make their appearance; pass, re-pass, glide away, and mingle in an infinite variety of postures and situations. There is properly no *simplicity* in it at one time, nor *identity* in different; whatever natural propension we may have to imagine that simplicity and identity. The comparison of the theatre must not

mislead us. They are the successive perceptions only, that constitute the mind; nor have we the most distant notion of place, where these scenes are represented . . . (T 253).

Hume's point is that we regard the mind as the stage or the uniting ground for all of our changing experiences, and yet we have no perception to which we can trace that idea of the mind. What we call the mind is in fact a series of passing perceptions, like the changing scenes and actors in a theatre, but the imagination disguises this, and we think of a single, simply entity.

Hume asks: "What then gives us so great a propension to ascribe an identity to these successive perceptions, and to suppose ourselves possest of an invariable and uninterrupted existence thro' the whole course of our lives?" (T 253). We have already heard the story of our coming to believe in external objects because of our propensity to ascribe identity--the uninterruptedness of an object through time--to diversity--several resembling objects over time or simultaneously. But there is a special puzzle here: The same perceptions that play a part in our coming to believe in external objects are involved in our coming to a notion of the *subject* of the experiences, the self. How do the same perceptions lead one way, and the other?

Ascriptions of Identity

Hume maintains that all identity ascriptions, whether it is to plants and animals or to the self, are really ascriptions to series of related objects, rather than to a single object. He makes several observations about our tendency to attribute identity to diversity. First, he has us consider what we might say about a set of contiguous perceptions to which we have attributed an identity, but which undergoes some noticeable change. Take the ceramic coffee cup on my shelf: Let's say I arrive one day to find a coffee cup, which looks like the previous one, but with a chipped lip. In other words, my perceptions lose some degree of resemblance, which is key in our individuation of objects. Do we call it the same cup? Of course we do, since the change is not so great as to make it unrecognizable. As Hume notes, what we do depends on the proportion of change relative to the object: The addition of a mountain to a planet would not cause us to believe we had a new planet before us, but a couple of inches added to a lady bug would make us wonder what new species we had. The psychological principle at work here seems to be that perceptual objects operate on the mind according to their proportion to each other, rather than according to any absolute size (T 256). If the changes are small relative to the previous perception, then the mind proceeds unimpeded in its progress of thought, and the change does not destroy the opinion of identity.

A second, related principle Hume finds at work in identity ascriptions is that where a change in a body occurs gradually, we are apt to consider it the same object (T 256). The wax of a lit candle melts gradually, and the mind has an easy time passing from perception to perception and supposes no interruption in the object. Were we to see the candle as dark red and a foot tall in one moment and then as mauve and three inches tall at another, we would not so easily assume that we were looking at the same candle.

A third condition under which the mind posits identity of a changing chain of perceptions is when we find a "*sympathy* of parts to their *common end*." This is the case with a ship in which many of its parts have been replaced. Even though it is largely made of new materials, we call it the same ship because the parts function with each other to produce a floating vessel. Likewise, an oak sapling that grows into a large tree has parts with a mutual dependence and connection that leads us to regard it as the same plant and talk about its growth, rather than to regard it as series of new plants.

Personal Identity

Hume says that the same principles that operate to produce our ideas of external objects are at work in producing the idea of the self. We know there are three relations that obtain among our perceptions, and so, only these three--contiguity, resemblance, and causation--can cause us to unite the varied perceptions into one. Hume rules out contiguity as having a part in our attributions of personal identity, apparently thinking it obvious why. Perhaps his reasoning is that perceptions contiguous in time and space only get us to the notion of objects.[1] To consider how the other two relations work, Hume has us imagine we can look into the mind of another (over time) and asks us to examine what we find there. The third person perspective must not be crucial in this experiment; if it were, Hume's account would give one no conclusions about the idea of oneself, but only about ideas of other minds. So, to perform this experiment, I could be looking into my own mind, or you into yours.

We look inside a mind, and we find passing perceptions, of course, but do we find relationships between any of them? First of all, some are related by resemblance: Some ideas resemble impressions, and some ideas resemble other ideas. The more vivacious of these ideas count as memories, on Hume's characterization of memory (see chapter 1). Substantial portions of what we find in one's mind are memories, and memories presumably will be resemblances of other perceptions; so we find a large number of resembling perceptions. Here we have one relation that accounts for the mind's finding identity among the diversity, and some philosophers, like John Locke, have argued that the self is defined by its memories. Hume maintains, however, that resemblance is not enough to account entirely for the way in which we think of ourselves. I regard myself as the same person I was in infancy, even though I have no memories of that time. And there may be periods of my life of which I have no memories now, because memories fade, and yet I don't regard myself as going out of existence when that happens. How so? Causality, Hume says, is the relation that allows us to extend identity beyond memory. I find among these perceptions some causally related to others--impressions cause ideas, and ideas cause other ideas and passions. The imagination "bundles" these related perceptions into the idea of a self. For instance, say that I've felt uneasy around my uncle for my whole life, but I don't know why. Someone looking into my perceptions finds a causal connection between that feeling and an experience I had at a very young age, which I don't now remember. That causal connection is a basis for the imagination's tying the notion of my self to that experience. But since the idea of self or person is not traceable directly to experience, but is instead the effect on the imagination of relations between perceptions, it is another fiction.

Some Comments on the Account

(1) How is it that the same set of perceptions carries us to the idea of object as well as to the idea of subject? The constancy and coherence of perceptions lead us one way; the resemblance and causality between them lead the other. But constancy of perceptions is nothing but the repeated occurrence of resembling perceptions. So, how do resembling perceptions lead us both outward and inward? The answer is that Hume's generic term "perception" includes both impressions and ideas, and it is important to distinguish the two here. Resembling, or constant,

impressions lead to the notion of an outward object, one causing the impressions and keeping the qualities in existence when not perceived. On the other hand, *ideas* resembling impressions, or *ideas* resembling other ideas leads to the notion of the person or mind who has the ideas.

(2) Even though Hume's argument concerning the derivation of the idea of a person is meant to apply to my perspective on myself, the argument has the appearance of circularity when put in the first person. Consider: "If *I* observe the contents of *my* mind, *I* find that some of *my* perceptions are related by resemblance and some by causality; on the basis of these relationships, *my* mind conjures up the notion of *my* self." Hume's account requires that a mind do the introspection that produces the data on which the idea of the mind is based. So, the account of how we acquire an idea of the mind presupposes the existence of a mind.[2] But the question crucial to circularity is really this: Do I have to be aware of myself (of my mind) when I do the introspection and posit the idea of self? For only if this were the case would there be a circularity in Hume's argument; then, we would need the *concept* of the self to derive the concept. But Hume's account does not assume the concept, as far as I can tell. As Hume himself says, we always presuppose the existence of objects, even though we cannot prove they exist. No doubt he would say the same about the self.

(3) There is still good reason to question the correctness of his account of personal identity, however. Suppose all the perceptions ever had in the universe are spilt out before us. We trace the relations of resemblance and causation the best we can, and group the perceptions into selves on that basis. Would we really be able to derive ideas of all the persons we now think there are? Consider shared experiences that produce resembling perceptions in different people; how would we bundle these? What about perceptions of one person that are causally connected to perceptions of another? For instance, I hear a car horn and I'm startled; then you're jarred by my sudden jerk. Chains of resembling perceptions and causally connected perceptions seem to cross person boundaries. This fact indicates that Hume has not really captured the criterion of individuation we actually use, whatever it might be.[3]

Fictions and Humean Skepticism

Hume concludes that we have ideas of external objects and of the self and of other persons, but that these ideas have a special status. He has argued earlier that all meaningful ideas begin in experience, but now he has unearthed some notions we regularly use that cannot be traced to experience. He doesn't conclude, however, that his original theory of ideas was wrong, but rather, that we have to dig more deeply into the principles of the mind to reveal the nature of these ideas. It does follow from his theory, however, that these ideas are ones whose significance we really don't understand. He calls them "fictions."

Hume doesn't mean that fictions are false beliefs, although they do seem to depend on some false beliefs. One plausible way to construe a fiction is as an idea applied to a thing from which it was not derived.[4] For instance, while the imagination creates the notion of the external world to deal with a kind of psychological conflict, we apply the idea to experience, as though we found external objects there in the first place. Hume is not suggesting that we eliminate the use of fictions, given that fictions arise in us spontaneously. He is, though, critical of the fictions of philosophers, since these notions do not naturally come to us on our own. While the fictions of the vulgar are what we all believe naturally, why would anyone believe in double existence, or in "substance," the philosophers' term for the reality that binds together experienced qualities, but is not itself experienced? Yet, these fictions are supposed to solve problems generated by the views of the ordinary person!

It is worth noting that, at the end of his discussion of the external world and the self, Hume sounds less a naturalist and more a skeptic than ever before. He admits to having begun his discussion intending to conclude that we should have faith in the workings of the mind; now he concludes with an attitude of mistrust: "I cannot conceive how such trivial qualities of the fancy [the imagination], conducted by such false suppositions, can ever lead to any solid and rational system" (T 217). On the other hand, drawing the skeptical conclusion that none of the human faculties is trustworthy is self-defeating. On this view, reason itself cannot be trusted, and there is no method for philosophy to follow. Hume finds this a depressing place to end up. What now?

> Most fortunately it happens, that since reason is incapable of dispelling these clouds, nature herself suffices to that purpose, and cures me of this philosophical melancholy and delirium, either by relaxing this bent of mind, or by some avocation, and lively impression of my senses, which obliterate all these chimeras. I dine, I play a game of back-gammon, I converse, and am merry with my friends; . . . (T 269)

Hume confesses then that when he tires of amusement, he is ready to go back to intellectual pursuits, but this time enquiring into practical matters--the principles of morality, the foundation of government, the passions. And here he recommends philosophy again, as an antidote to the superstition some people carry into these inquires. Superstition, he says, can lead to dangerous beliefs, while bad philosophy only looks ridiculous (T270-72)! So the question addressed in Chapter 2, to what degree Hume is a skeptic and to what degree a naturalist, arises again.[5]

Discussion Questions

1. What is the difference between a continued existence and a distinct existence, and how are they related?
2. What do Hume's accounts of coming to a belief in the external world and coming to an idea of the self have in common?
3. In his theory of ideas, Hume claims that the imagination rearranges ideas derived from the senses into patterns in which they did not first come--for example attaching a lion's head to a horse. Is this depiction of the imagination consistent with his discussion of the work of the imagination in producing fictions, ideas that do not come directly from experience?

Endnotes

1. Contiguous perceptions are perceptions occurring together or in sequence. Perhaps Hume's thinking is that perceptions in different minds are contiguous. You and I are having all sorts of perceptions at the same time or in sequence; so, contiguity can't be helpful in individuating persons.
2. Stroud seems to think this is more problematic; see his pp. 130-33.
3. Later, in the Appendix to the *Treatise*, 633-36, Hume expresses doubts about the success of his account of personal identity. I regret that I don't have the space to discuss his afterthoughts.
4. See Saul Traiger, "Impressions, Fictions, and Ideas," *Hume Studies* 13 (Nov. 1987): 381-399.
4. For more on this debate, see Chapter 4 of Don Garrett, *Cognition and Commitment in Hume's Philosophy* (Oxford, 1997).

4

The Psychology
of the Passions

The Division of our Passions

We know that Hume's theory of ideas divides our most vivid
perceptions into impressions of sensation and impressions of reflection.
We have seen how our impressions of sensation are involved in our
causal beliefs and in our beliefs in the existence of the physical world.
Hume is also interested in examining our impressions of reflection--our
passions, or emotions, or feelings. We should recall that impressions of
reflection are experiences, which result from reflecting on the sources
of our pleasures and pains, which are themselves sensations. For
instance, if I regularly feel pleasure in someone's company and reflect
on aspects of my friend's personality that I enjoy, I acquire an emotion:
a feeling of love toward a good friend of mine. On the other hand, if I
feel uncomfortable (a sort of pain) at the achievements of a co-worker
and reflect on her accomplishments, I may develop a passion of envy or
of resentment. Since human beings normally enjoy pleasurable
experiences and shun painful ones, feelings of pleasure and pain
somehow underlie what prompts us to act; hence, it makes sense that
Hume's discussion of the passions eventually leads to the topic of
motivation to action.

In his psychology of the passions, Hume draws two important
distinctions that result in a classification of the passions. First, he
notices that some passions are *calm* and some are *violent*. This is a
rough distinction based on the way emotions feel to us: Some are felt in

a "soft" manner and are sometimes barely perceptible; others come over us with a great force and intensity. Among the calm passions, Hume says, are the sense of beauty and the sense of morality. Among the violent passions are other feelings, such as "love and hatred, grief and joy, pride and humility" (T 276).

Consider the calm passions. We react emotionally to our thoughts of objects, of nature, and of persons, and we make judgments of beauty and of morality based on our responses. In the case of judgments of beauty, we regard this ability to react as our sense of beauty; in the case of judgements of the morality of persons' characters, we regard this capacity as our moral sense. Hume characterizes these passions as "calm," since he thinks they are typically felt in a subdued way and even often mistaken with the "feeling" of reason. This is so, because someone in rational contemplation or reflection is typically unperturbed and relaxed; but so is someone who experiences a calm passion. So, for instance, when I react to the roses in my garden, I feel a kind of calm pleasure in their presence, which is connected to my perception of their beauty. This leads some to argue--mistakenly, Hume thinks--that aesthetic judgments and moral judgments are formulated by reason. (We will take a close look at his theory of morality in the next chapter.)

On the other hand, if I take pride in my roses because they are beautiful and because I cultivated them myself, that pride, Hume contends, is felt with a sort of forcefulness that prompts him to consider pride a violent passion. And so it goes for the other violent passions: My hatred, for example, of a malicious serial killer is felt forcefully, and so Hume considers it a violent passion. It is not clear that Hume's distinction between calm and violent passions is based on the force and vivacity dimension with which he distinguishes impressions from ideas, but they surely are similar. Still, all passions, being impressions rather than ideas, have more force and vivacity than any ideas do, no matter whether we're talking about a calm passion or a violent one.

The second distinction Hume makes among our passions is between the *direct* and the *indirect* passions. This distinction plays a larger role in his theory than the former one between the calm and the violent, since it is a distinction concerned with how the respective types of passions are produced. Furthermore, how they are produced apparently determines whether they serve as motives to action, even though Hume never says so explicitly. But when he discusses motives to action, he always discusses direct passions.

The direct passions are those which arise immediately from reflection on pleasures and pains, without the need to call upon other perceptions. What this means is more easily explained after we have an account of the opposite set, the indirect passions, before us. Among the direct passions Hume lists desire, aversion, grief, joy, hope, fear, despair, and security. The indirect passions, on the other hand, are those which are caused in us by reflection on pleasure and pain, but in cooperation with other perceptions. Among these are pride, humility, ambition, vanity, love, hatred, envy, pity, malice, and generosity.

The Indirect Passions

In exploring Hume's explanation of how we acquire the indirect passions, it is important to bear in mind his goal as a natural scientist of accounting for the activities of the human mind in as few principles as possible. When he asks what causes a passion like pride or humility, he wants to know whether there is something all similar passions have in common that allows a general explanation of how they are produced. Were each one produced from an "original" cause, we would have no general principles by which to explain the generation of the indirect passions. But he does find something the causes of these passions have in common and on which their causal influence depends, namely, "a double relation of impressions and ideas." To understand what Hume means, we first have to recall a key feature of human nature--the tendency of the mind to associate ideas by the principles of resemblance, contiguity, and cause and effect. Likewise, Hume says, the mind passes from one passion, or impression of reflection, to another, based on a resemblance of feeling:

> Grief and disappointment give rise to anger, anger to envy, envy to malice, and malice to grief again, till the whole circle be compleated. In like manner our temper, when elevated with joy, naturally throws itself into love, generosity, pity, courage, pride, and the other resembling affections (T 283).

Hume uses this principle of association of the passions in his account of the causes of the indirect passions.

Pride and Humility

Consider, first, the cause of the indirect passion of pride. In the most general terms, one has pride when something reflects well on

49

oneself. Hume observes that pride is always caused by our thinking of a subject that is (a) related to the self and (b) has a pleasing quality. Both are necessary. I take pride in my abundant garden, my beautiful pottery, my talented offspring. If the quality weren't pleasant--if it were a dying garden, a lopsided pot, or an ill-mannered child--I wouldn't take pride in the subject. And if the subject weren't related to me--if it were someone else's garden, some stranger's pottery, or the child of a distant acquaintance--I wouldn't feel proud of the subject. We know, then, that the cause of pride is an idea and it has two parts, a quality and a subject. In "my abundant garden," the subject is the garden and the quality is its abundance. In "my talented offspring," the subject is my child and the quality is her being talented. Further, we know that the idea of the quality causes pleasure, and that the idea of the subject is related to an idea of the self. In the example of the garden, the thought of abundance is pleasurable, and the idea of the garden is related to me by causality (I produced it) or by ownership (it is mine). In the example of my child, the thought of her talents is pleasurable, and the idea of my child is related to me by causality (I produced her).

Now consider the passion of pride itself. Hume finds two qualities in the feeling of pride. The first is that the object of pride is the self. I can be proud of my children, just as I can be proud of my garden, but that makes my children the subject of pride, not the object. Pride is a passion that always leads the mind to an idea of the self, and in that respect, the self is its object. Hume emphasizes that nature has "assigned" the idea of self to this passion, in the same respect that the idea of food always accompanies the sensation of hunger (T 287). The second feature of pride Hume observes is that pride is itself a pleasurable feeling. All emotions are somehow based on, or even manifestations of, pleasures and pains, and it makes no sense to identify an emotion as pride if it is connected to pain. We must note that the pleasure of pride is a separate feeling of pleasure from the pleasure one takes in the quality of the subject that causes pride.

Consequently, Hume explains the production of pride in terms of what he calls a double relation of impressions and ideas. The cause of pride (quality plus subject) is associated with an idea of the self and causes an impression of pleasure. The effect, namely pride itself, is also associated with an idea of the self and produces a separate impression of pleasure. Since the human mind is disposed to move from one perception to another that resembles it, these relationships facilitate the formation of the passion in the following way. When I think of my beautiful pottery, the idea of myself, which I associate with the pottery, transports my mind to the idea of the self that is the object of the passion of pride (an association of ideas); likewise, the pleasure I take in the beautiful quality of the pottery moves my mind along to the similar sensation of pleasure that is essential to pride (an association of impressions). The cause is doubly related to the effect, and both lines of mental association contribute to the generation of the passion of pride. In sum: "Any thing, that gives a pleasant sensation, and is related to self, excites the passion of pride, which is also agreeable, and has self for its object" (T 288).

The account goes similarly for the other indirect passions. Humility is the opposite of pride, and the two are often treated as a pair. What pride and humility have in common is that each has the self as object. But whereas pride is a pleasurable passion, humility is a painful one. Their subjects are similar in being associated with the self, but dissimilar in that the quality of the subject of humility produces displeasure. For instance, I hear a displeasing voice on a tape recorder and then discover it's mine. I feel humiliated due to the fact that the cause, the voice, is associated with me, and its distasteful quality causes me pain. This idea of my self, the possessor of that voice, leads my mind to the idea of the self, the object of humility, and the pain provoked in me resembles the pain of the passion. In humility, a displeasurable quality of a subject related to me produces the passion, which is itself displeasurable and has my self as object. So, the analysis of humility parallels that of pride.

Love and Hatred

The other pair of indirect passions Hume analyzes is love and hatred. Love and hatred differ from pride and humility in that the object of the former is always, Hume says, some other person, that is, someone, unlike the self, of whose thoughts, actions, and sensations we are not directly aware. Hume writes,

> Our love and hatred are always directed to some sensible being external to us; and when we talk of *self-love*, 'tis not in a proper sense, nor has the sensation it produces anything in common with that tender emotion, which is excited by a friend or mistress. 'Tis the same case with hatred. We may be mortified by our own faults and follies; but never feel any anger or hatred, except from the injuries of others (T 329-30).

51

While the affections we feel for others surely do feel differently from self-love, one may wonder whether genuine anger or hatred might at times be directed at the self. Furthermore, even though Hume excludes self-love and self-hatred from the classes of emotions he is describing, what Hume means here by love and by hatred actually includes broader categories of emotions than we ordinarily include under these terms.

Hume notes that many qualities prompt love and many prompt hatred. I may love someone for his or her wit, good sense, sense of humor, virtue, knowledge, beauty, or dexterity, but I might also love someone for his or her property and riches or heritage, he says. Conversely, I may hate someone for having the opposite traits, for being dull, frivolous, or vicious, or for being ugly or poor. The sorts of passions of which Hume writes here are not narrowly confined to the type of love felt toward a friend or a marriage partner, or to the type of hatred felt toward an enemy or a lover who spurned one. Love includes the emotions of esteem and respect; hatred includes feelings of contempt and disrespect (T 357). We might protest that another's appearance or wealth or social standing is no proper cause of love or hatred, but we also have to remember that Hume is describing human nature, rather than prescribing what would make it better. It does not seem far-fetched to think that people typically admire the rich, famous, and beautiful over the ordinary person.

A double relation of impressions and ideas also produces love and hatred. The cause of love is a pleasing quality of a subject related to another person; the love produced in the admirer is also pleasurable and has the other person as its object. For instance, I love my best friend for her kind disposition and good humor. The love is facilitated by those traits' relation to my friend and by the pleasure her traits produce in me. They occasion a pleasurable passion, love, which has her as the object. Of course, hatred happens in a parallel manner, with the difference being that the quality of the subject (cause) is displeasing, as is the feeling of hatred itself.

An interesting feature of love and hatred that Hume observes and analyzes is that each is accompanied by another passion, while pride and humility are not. Love is always attended with a desire for the happiness of the beloved and an aversion to his or her misery; hatred is always accompanied by a desire for misery of the person despised and an aversion to that person's happiness. The one passion Hume calls benevolence, and the other he calls anger. What makes this discussion more significant is that Hume asserts that pride and humility and love and hatred are not themselves motives to action, while benevolence and

52

anger are. So, we always possess motivating passions along with love and hatred. What is a motivating passion, and why is this important?

One of the reasons Hume studies the psychology of the passions is to set the stage for a discussion of actions and morality. In turning the discussion from what we know to how we feel, Hume has moved into the area of practical philosophy. Whereas his theory of ideas and his analysis of belief have no direct implications for behavior (I don't give up believing even if Hume is right that belief about the world involves fictions), the theory of the passions does have practical implications. The passions are our feelings, and one of the theses for which Hume argues vigorously (see below, in this chapter) is that feelings are necessary to produce actions. His view, which many other philosophers and ordinary folks share, is that attractions to some things and aversions away from others are ultimately the causes of our actions. These attractions and aversions are the causes of our actions because they prompt us toward the objects that appeal to us and away from the ones that repulse us. Causes of actions are called motives; when we ask what motivated an action, we want to know what caused the agent to do it. Hence, these attractions and aversions that cause actions are motives to action. But attractions and aversions simply are feelings or passions; so, at least some passions are motives. The study of morality, that area of thought dealing with norms for behavior, is connected to a study of passions, then. If all actions begin in motives and motives are passions, then if moral norms regulate actions, they must affect our passions.

It is important to understand in this discussion that when Hume talks about motives like benevolence and anger, he is talking about the mental states that are candidates for causing action, but they don't always cause actions. One may have a motive and not act on it. I may desire the bad fortune of a person I despise without acting on that desire. After all, it may conflict with other, stronger motives I possess, such as kindness or a sense of right and wrong, which prompts me away from doing harm to other people. All actions have motives, but not all motives result in actions; motives are "urges," but we don't always act on them--namely, when other, competing urges are stronger.

So love and hatred are special among the indirect passions because they always occur naturally with the motives of benevolence and anger, respectively. But what is the evidence that there are four feelings present, rather than just two? Why isn't love simply desiring the good of another, and hatred desiring the unhappiness or bad fortune of another? Hume's answer is the good empiricist's reply: We can conceive of love without benevolence and hatred without anger; if they are separable in thought, they are different mental states. We know that desire for the good of another only arises upon the thought of the other's good, and we can very well feel love for someone before their good comes to mind. We can also very well hate another before we think of what is contrary to their interest. So, love and hatred can well exist without their accompanying motives, even though the motives will occur eventually. And, he adds, it is only a contingent fact that love is accompanied by benevolence and hatred by anger; there is nothing in the notions of these feelings that make it impossible for nature to have arranged it so that other desires might have arisen instead (T 367-68). It is simply a fact of our nature that these do.

The Direct Passions

The direct passions are those which arise immediately from feelings of pleasure and pain. (Hume later adds a qualification to this definition, which we will consider momentarily.) This means that the direct passions occur with no introduction of an idea of self or others; we simply feel a certain way about an object that causes us pleasure or about one that causes us pain. Among the direct passions, according to Hume, are desire and aversion, grief and joy, hope and fear. Because we have a natural proclivity for pleasurable things and a natural aversion toward painful ones, when we acquire a direct passion, we acquire a motive toward or away from an object. In other words, the direct passions are motives to action.

Let's consider some examples. I enjoy the taste of chocolate ice cream, and so, I want some chocolate ice cream now. The death of my aunt is painful, and so, I feel grief. The birth of my nephew is a pleasant prospect; so, I feel joy at my sister's announcement of her pregnancy. The response from the readers to my last article was pleasing to me; so, I hope for more of the same with my current writing. The comments from the reviewers, however, were unpleasant, and so, I fear more of their remarks on this piece. It's fairly easy to see how such passions arise directly from the feelings of pleasure and pain. These passions prompt us towards those things we find pleasant and away from those we find painful, although this doesn't mean we always act on the promptings. Even though I am averse to thoughts of my aunt's death, I attend my aunt's funeral because my respect for her outweighs my aversion. And even though I desire it, I don't eat all the chocolate ice cream in sight, because I have other strong, contrary motivations, like the desire for good health.

54

Hume adds an exception to his general description of the direct passions when he writes,

> Besides good and evil, or in other words, pain and pleasure, the direct passions frequently arise from a natural impulse or instinct, which is perfectly unaccountable. Of this kind is the desire of punishment to our enemies, and of happiness to our friends; hunger, lust, and a few other bodily appetites. These passions, properly speaking, produce good and evil, and proceed not from them, like the other affections (T 439).

Here, as in many other contexts, Hume equates pleasure with natural good and pain with natural evil (what is morally good and evil might be something else). For some reason, he thinks the direct passions he mentions above cannot be explained by the general principles that explain the other direct passions, namely, their proceeding directly from pleasure or pain. We simply have them. Elsewhere, he adds to this list of unaccountable passions benevolence and resentment, love of life, and kindness to children (T 417). But why are these unaccountable?

Hume seems to have in mind something along the following lines. People who are benevolent desire the good of others, even when others are not necessarily the source of pleasure to them. They just desire it. And people who love life just love it, regardless of whether it has a preponderance of pleasure over pain, or vice versa. People who are kind to children are simply that way, regardless of whether they even know the children to whom they are moved to be kind. Hunger originates in me, not from my perception of pleasure or pain from another object. And so on for the other "original instincts."

The Theory of Motivation

A long-standing debate among philosophers asks: Are we moral only in so far as we listen to reason and overcome many of our own passions, or do the passions have a place in the moral life? Hume's psychological study paves the way to an answer, since understanding how we are motivated to act is a first step to understanding what sort of norms could possibly affect, change, or regulate our behavior. Since we think of moral values or moral rules as having an affect on our behavior, whatever moral values and norms are, they must be the sort of thing to which human behavior is responsive. Hume has already intimated that he thinks all behavior is motivated by passions (which implies that morality must work on the passions to affect behavior). But he must be able to defend this view against the popular theory that motivation can be supplied by reason without the passions. As Hume says, it is very common for people to talk of the combat of reason and passion and to think that they are virtuous when they conform their behavior to the dictates of reason (T 413). The view is that if we reflect on morality, we will be able to infer what we are supposed to be, or how we're supposed to live. In other words, the basic principles of morality are rational ones. Once we discover them, the expectation is that they will affect our motivations, but that our passions can thwart our doing what reason tells us to do. This theory is found among the Ancients[1] and among Hume's contemporaries,[2] but Hume thinks it is mistaken on two counts. He will show (1) that reason alone can never be a motive to action, and (2) that reason can never oppose passion over the direction of action. The debate whether the dictates of morality come to us from reason Hume treats in a later discussion; the issue of what can motivate us is a step toward making his case about that issue.

Reason Alone Doesn't Motivate

Hume's argument why reason alone can never be a motive to action is the following. We know now that "reason" can refer to one of two ways of connecting ideas: demonstration or causal reasoning (see Chapter 2 here). He considers each in turn.

Demonstration is deductive reasoning using relations of ideas, and relations of ideas are the necessary truths that state how our concepts are related--for instance, a square is not a circle, and four plus five equals nine. Since demonstration is about concepts, regardless of whether anything exists in the world, Hume argues that it cannot motivate us to action, since action has to do with our intention of changing the way we perceive things to be in the world. Mathematics can be applied to the world in the way that mechanics or merchants use it to solve problems in their work, but knowing the truths of mathematics only, without the addition of a goal or purpose, will not produce an impulse to act.

Can causal reasoning by itself give us a motive, an urge or a push, to action? Remember, causal reasoning concerns purported connections in the world and allows us to form beliefs about the way the world is. Do these matter-of-fact beliefs that come from causal reasoning supply us with motivation to act in particular ways? Consider some examples: I believe the weather is rainy. It seems this belief can motivate me to carry an umbrella when I go outdoors. I've just exercised and I believe there is cold water in the refrigerator. It seems this belief can motivate me to go to the refrigerator, take the water out, and drink it. If so, causal reasoning can on its own give me motives. But Hume notices that such beliefs would have no practical effect on us if we didn't also have some sort of attraction to the goal achieved by the motivated action--staying dry in the rainy weather and quenching my thirst after exercise. He traces this attraction to a familiar aspect of our nature--the propensity for pleasure and the aversion to pain. Getting wet in a downpour on the way to work is unpleasant; I have to be in damp clothes and feel cold all day. Being thirsty after exercise is unpleasant, too, and drinking water when my mouth is parched is a great pleasure.

Hume thinks we can be fooled by the fact that when we are attracted to something, reasoning figures out what is connected to that object; then, our attraction is extended to the other things related by causality to the original object. It looks as though reason is initiating the attraction, when in fact it only gives us information about causal connections. If I don't want to get wet in the rain, reason informs me that taking an umbrella with me is a way to achieve my goal; but reason didn't tell me what ends or goals to have. It simply gives me this piece of causal information: Staying under cover of an umbrella keeps one dry. Likewise, causal reasoning can tell me how to quench my thirst, but it doesn't give me the original desire to drink. Hume writes,

'Tis from the prospect of pleasure or pain that the aversion or propensity arises toward any object: And these emotions extend themselves to the causes and effects of that object, as they are pointed out to us by reason and experience. It can never in the least concern us to know, that such objects are causes, and such other effects, if both the causes and effects be indifferent to us. Where the objects themselves do not affect us, their connexion can never give them any influence; and 'tis plain, that as reason is nothing but the discovery of this connexion, it cannot be by its means that the objects are able to affect us (T 414).

Causal beliefs have no influence on our behavior if they are about things in the world of no concern to us. It doesn't affect me in a practical way to know that there is an eight-hour time difference between my home in California and London, England, unless I have a stake in an activity connected to that piece of information. The point is that I must have a concern, an interest, an attraction, etc., that makes a piece of factual information relevant to my behavior before it can play any part in motivating me. We have already encountered Hume's answer to the question in what that concern or motivation originates, namely, a passion. The direct passions, we know, either follow immediately upon pleasure and pain, or else they are instinctive propensities that produce pleasure or pain. My fear of getting wet in the rain is an example of the former; my thirst is an example of the latter. The fear, the thirst and like passions provide the necessary impetus that a belief produced by reason cannot provide.

Reason Versus Passion?

The second thesis for which Hume argues in connection with motivation is that reason and passion can never oppose each other over the direction of a person's action. A common view is that reason might tell us, say, to pay off our debts before buying anything else we don't really need, while passion urges us to buy this new stereo system now. Hume thinks there is a logical mistake in this view, that reason is not the sort of thing that can oppose passion. First, he asks what is necessary for something to be opposed to passion. Passion produces an impetus, an internal force, to motion. The only way something can be opposed to passion is by initiating a motivation in a contrary direction. But we have seen that reason cannot initiate a motivation at all. If reason cannot originate an impetus to action, it is equally incapable of opposing an impetus that already comes from a passion (T 414 -15).

Another way to get to the same conclusion is to ask what is necessary for something to oppose reason. Hume defines reason as the discovery of truth and falsity, which is a way of saying that reason gives us mental states that have cognitive content--that is, that contain information, or represent the way the world is. Reason gives us beliefs, and beliefs can represent truthfully or falsely. So, something that opposes reason must have cognitive content as well, and present information contrary to some belief rendered by reason. But, Hume argues, passions do not represent anything: "A passion is an original existence, or, if you will, modification of existence, and contains not any representative quality . . . " (T415). My anger does not represent to me a state of affairs (even though it may be based on a belief about what someone has done) any more than my hunger or thirst does.

But, Hume's opponent asks, aren't you feeling an unreasonable emotion when you are, say, angry, at someone who has really done nothing to offend you? Hume does admit that we have a non-technical way of speaking about emotions and we accept this talk in ordinary conversation. At the same time, as philosophers, we have to recognize that it is not an exact way of speaking. We tend to call a passion unreasonable when it is accompanied by false belief, and this might happen in one of two ways: (1) When a passion is founded on the supposition of objects that actually do not exist; and (2) when we do bad causal reasoning about the means to the end given by the passion and fix on an insufficient means to our goal (T 416). Consider examples of each. (1) A child reads about unicorns in her storybooks and hopes someday to see one. She has a hope, one of the Humean passions, founded on a false supposition of existence. It is the existence belief that, properly speaking, is unreasonable, though. (2) I desire (another passion) to find a bargain on furniture and I set my sights on the most upscale furniture store in town, not realizing that it doesn't offer bargain prices. Here I have chosen an insufficient means to my ends because I have a false belief. But the desire to go to this store is not in itself irrational; Hume says that the belief is.

But here is another challenge to Hume: If the impetus to action always originates with a passion, then why does it look as though beliefs, which come from reason, can sometimes make our passions come and go? And if beliefs can make passions come and go, then they really do initiate motivation--by controlling our passions. For instance, I have a craving for my favorite sandwich and go to the deli next door to my office to get one. The clerk there tells me, to my disappointment, that the sandwich has been taken off the menu. So I change my choice, in light of that information, to a different sandwich in the shop. A mother fears that her child has been kidnapped from the mall when he turns up missing; her fears are turned to joy when the police phone her with the information that he has been found uninjured at a nearby park. In both cases, it looks as though beliefs are manipulating the passions.

Hume is emphatic that this is not the case: "Reason is, and ought only to be the slave of the passions, and can never pretend to any other office than to serve and obey them" (T 415). How is this so, when it looks as though beliefs are changing our passions? First, remember, Hume himself emphasizes that beliefs are practical and have an impact on our emotions (see Chapter 2 here), just as the case of fear turned to joy illustrates. Nonetheless, he doesn't see this point as inconsistent with his general view that reason services the passions. This is because, in any case, we will always find some initial passions, originated in the way direct passions are (i.e., without reason), with which beliefs work. My craving for my favorite sandwich doesn't necessarily vanish upon my realizing it no longer exists. But my choice of an alternative is explained by my general appetite for food, which is fulfilled by my settling upon something else offered in the deli. In other words, my belief about what sandwiches are available serves my general desire to eat. In the case of a mother's fear turned to joy, she would experience neither passion if she didn't first care for her child's welfare. Her beliefs affect her emotions only because she has an underlying passion, itself not originated by reason. Hume believes that if we look deeply enough, we will always discover passions at the source of our actions.[3]

Some Remarks on Hume's Theory of Motivation

A startling implication of Hume's theory of motivation is that it makes no sense, strictly speaking, to call actions rational or irrational. Since they are caused by passions, which cannot be so evaluated, there is no basis on which to apply the terms to actions. This is not to say, however, that actions are subject to no evaluations whatsoever, since they are objects of moral judgment, as we shall see in the next chapter.

In discussions of motivation, Hume's view, that reason gives us only factual beliefs that help us figure out how to get the objects of our passions, is called an "instrumentalist" theory of practical reasoning. Theories of practical reasoning concern how we reason about what we ought to do. Instrumentalism gets its name from its viewing the products of reason, namely beliefs, as instruments, or tools, that aid the passions in fulfilling their ends. But some philosophers would say that classifying instrumentalism as a theory of "practical" reasoning at all is inaccurate. Philosophers who believe that reason is practical in a more robust sense reject Hume's division of reason into demonstration and causal reasoning. Instead, they look at it this way: "Theoretical" reason gives us beliefs about conceptual relations and beliefs about the world (Hume's only two categories), and "practical" reason gives us conclusions about what we ought to do. When these philosophers say that practical reason tells us what we ought to do, they mean it tells us what ends to pursue, and not merely the means to the ends set by the passions. On Hume's view, reason never gives me a belief of the form, "I ought to pursue A;" rather, it gives us beliefs of the form, "X causes Y." If this information is useful in procuring the object of a passion, I may utilize it, but whether or not I do has nothing to do with rationality.

Hume's opponents are committed to evaluating actions by two standards they see as derived from reason: the moral and the prudential. Since Hume treats morality in a separate discussion, it is best to set that topic aside for now. But his theory of motivation has something to say about prudence. Everyone agrees that prudence is that trait which makes one look after one's long-term self-interest. So, it is prudent to do some things that I really don't like in this moment--getting a root canal or doing my exercises--because I am better off in the long run for doing them. Many philosophers take for granted that doing what is in one's long-term self-interest, being prudent, is rational, and acting contrary to long-term self-interest is not. After all, long-term self-interest conduces to survival with a certain quality of life, a natural goal of living things. So, practical rationality, on this view, is designed (in part) to tell us what we ought to do to fulfill our long-term self-interest. (It is also supposedly designed to tell us what we ought to do, morally-speaking.) But Hume's reply is this:

> 'Tis not contrary to reason to prefer the destruction of the whole world to the scratching of my finger. 'Tis not contrary to reason for me to chuse my total ruin, to prevent the least uneasiness of an *Indian* or person wholly unknown to me. 'Tis as little contrary to reason to prefer even my own acknowledged lesser good to my greater . . . (T 416).

Why does Hume make these dramatic remarks? His response here to his opponents follows consistently from the conclusion he has already defended: Preferences (passions) are never contrary to reason, no matter what preferences they are, and neither are the actions we do in light of them. This is not to say that preferring the destruction of the world over getting a scratch on my finger is not evil, but it is not the sort of thing that can be evaluated by reason (which means that whether something is good or evil is not set by reason either, as we shall see).

Freedom and Necessity

A discussion of motivation to action prompts the question whether human beings are free. The dilemma of freedom and determinism has been with philosophy since its beginning. If all events in the universe are caused, and human actions are events, they are also caused. But we see causes as necessitating their effects; so, if our actions are caused, then we have to see them as necessitated, and it looks as though we must believe we could never do otherwise than we do. On the other hand, we believe ourselves to be free to choose what we do, which means that we think we could have done otherwise than what we in fact have done. But if we think we could have done otherwise, then we can't see our actions as caused. So, either human actions fit into our scientific view of the universe and we see ourselves as determined, or we believe in exceptions to natural law and see ourselves as free.

Hume has argued that the idea of necessity arises when we become accustomed to a constant conjunction of events and the mind is determined to pass from the perception of the one to an idea of the other. This is the way we see events in nature as necessitated, and Hume argues that when we look at ourselves, we will find similar constant conjunctions between motives or temperaments and actions. He can't look inside any person's mind to observe their motives; so, the correlations on which he bases his claim are correlations between group identities and actions. He argues that there are regularities in actions exhibited within nationalities, age groups, and genders. How far these regularities go is a matter of much debate, and some may argue that this approach results in dangerous stereotyping, but no doubt Hume is right about some correlations. The young tend to bold and reckless behavior, while the older tend to more sedate and less risky behavior. Women tend to communicate in ways distinct from men, and there is no doubt some correlation between sexual psychology and behavior. The point is that there are regularities in human nature that produce the same sort of causal inferences we make about events in the rest of nature. Thus, Hume argues: "The same experienc'd union has the same effect on the mind, whether the united objects be motives, volitions, and actions; or figure and motion" (T 406-07). We must see actions as caused.

On Hume's view (and others' as well), if our actions were not necessitated, they would be uncaused, and to be uncaused is to be random and left to chance (T 407). But if actions are mere chance events, then they are tied in no way to the person who performs them. If they are not caused by his or her motives (or by anything), then how can we connect them to the actor? If we say that the person's motives cause her actions, but nothing causes motives, then motives become inexplicable mental states over which nothing--not even the agent--has control. Perhaps Hume's conclusion is unsettling, but as someone who looks for explanations of events in terms of the natural world, Hume is drawing the proper conclusions.

He does allow that if someone were to define freedom in a way that does not entail lack of causality, then an argument that we are free

62

might be mounted. Say, if a free act is defined as an act a person can do if he or she chooses, it follows that actions are free.[4] This definition does not deny that choices are caused, and so it is compatible with Hume's arguments. But all actions begin in motives, and if Hume is right that motives arise in us in the natural ways he has described, then it makes no sense to say that we freely choose our motives. There is a sense in which our motives are determined by our natures, but most proponents of human freedom would reject this characterization as capturing what it is to see ourselves as free. Many philosophers have concluded that freedom is a mystery for which we can account only by rational speculation going beyond experience and the laws of nature.

Discussion Questions

1. Hume never explains why the direct passions are motives, but the indirect passions are not. Can you offer an explanation why he might think this?
2. What must Hume mean by a "motive" to action?
3. Explain the meaning of Hume's famous (and often misunderstood) remark that "reason is slave to the passions."

Endnotes

1. This theory is found in Plato, for one.
2. The early modern moral rationalists include Samuel Clarke and William Wollaston. Immanuel Kant later held this view as well.
3. For a different reading of Hume on this matter, see Chapter 7 of Annette Baier, *A Progress of Sentiments: Reflections on Hume's Treatise* (Harvard University Press, 1991).
4. He suggests this in the *Enquiry Concerning Human Understanding* (EHU 95), but not explicitly in the *Treatise*. His *Enquiry* account of the dilemma of freedom and determinism turns the issue into a verbal dispute: Whether we are free depends on how we define the terms. Perhaps his change of emphasis was an attempt to make his audience more receptive to the discussion in the *Enquiry*.

5

The Practice of Morality

Moral philosophy in the seventeenth and eighteenth centuries was embroiled in a debate over how we derive our moral distinctions: Do we make them by the rational part of our nature or by the sensitive? In other words, do we reason about the difference between right and wrong or good and bad, or do we (also) need to call upon feelings to know the difference? We might wonder why anyone would be concerned with this issue when what ultimately matters is just knowing what we ought to do. But the former question has implications for the latter. If we can use reason by itself to get to moral conclusions, then the nature of morality has to be something in the purview of reason, something that doesn't require experience of present states of affairs, but consists in universal and absolute rules. On the other hand, if feeling or perception is needed, then morality is something contingent and dependent, on either the way humans perceive and feel (the human constitution) or on the way the world is constructed (what is perceived). Such a discussion does not get us to the content of morality--for instance, whether it is wrong to tell a lie--but making progress on these issues gets us closer to particular answers. The particular questions are questions within morality or normative ethics, because they ask what the individual norms are and how they apply to cases. Questions about the nature of moral distinctions constitute metaethics, because they make inquiries about the whole practice of morality. Hume deals with the latter first and then proceeds to the former, and his answer to the one depends on the other.

Hume's way of putting the metaethical problem others are debating is: "Do we make the distinction between virtue and vice by means of our ideas or by means of our impressions?" "Virtue" and "vice" are the terms we use to talk about good and bad character traits. Hume thinks our moral evaluations are ultimately about character, even though we can only observe the actions of others, which we then take as signs of their motivations. In other words, character traits are motives--the motives one consistently acts on. Now, when Hume asks whether we distinguish virtue from vice by means of ideas or by means of impressions, he is not asking whether the idea of virtue or the idea of vice derives from experience; we already know that all legitimate ideas (non-fictions) originate in experience and are copies of impressions. He is asking instead whether, after we have acquired the ideas involved, our regarding, for instance, malice as vicious and kindness as virtuous, is something we do merely by the use of reason, or whether it requires experience. Do I regard malice vicious by simply considering the ideas of malice and vice, or does sensory input get me to that judgment?

Moral Distinctions not Made by Reason Alone

Samuel Clarke, in his Boyle Lectures (1705)[1], was one of the prominent rationalist philosophers who fits Hume's description of his opponents:

> Those who affirm that virtue is nothing but a conformity to reason; that there are eternal fitnesses and unfitnesses of things, which are the same to every rational being that considers them; that the immutable measures of right and wrong impose an obligation, not only on human creatures, but also on the Deity himself: . . . (T 456).

Clarke's notion is that the universe has a rational structure where certain events fit, and the contrary events do not. Actions contrary to reason are morally wrong. Since this structure is rational, it is discernable by reason. For instance, it is self-evident to reason that it is more fit to promote the welfare of all people than to destroy other people; and it is obvious to us, without experience, that it is more fit to save the life of an innocent person than to kill that person with no provocation. But Hume asks whether we can really make moral judgments by relying only on reason. He offers the following simple argument: (1) Reason alone never motivates. (2) Morals excite passions and produce or prevent actions; that is, they motivate. (3) Therefore, morality cannot be derived from reason alone (T 457). What support is there for each of the premises?

(1) We have already seen extensive arguments for the first claim in Hume's theory of motivation (Chapter 4), and Hume wants us to keep those arguments in mind here. In sum, reason doesn't motivate because it is that mental function which discovers truth and falsity and so gives us informative, or cognitive, states of mind: our beliefs about the world. But such information doesn't affect behavior until it connects with a passion, which is the impetus to action. So reason, by itself, cannot generate motives or produce actions.

(2) The second premise in Hume's argument against the moral rationalists says that "morals" affect our passions and our actions. However ambiguous the term "morals" here, what Hume must mean, in order to present a valid argument, is that, when we accept or acknowledge that a particular trait is virtuous or vicious, or an act right or wrong, it gives us an attraction to, or a repulsion away from, the trait or the action. In other words, our making of moral distinctions imparts motives. Moreover, Hume must mean here that our discerning right from wrong motivates *on its own*, and not in view of a desire one already has, such as the desire for others' approval. For in that case, the desire for approval, rather than morality, would be providing the impulse to action. If Hume's second premise were taken to mean that morality motivates by conjoining with such a desire, then his conclusion would not follow. In that case, one might argue: (A) While reason alone doesn't motivate, it can motivate by conjoining its product, a belief, with a desire; (B) moral distinctions motivate in the same way, by being joined with a pertinent desire; (C) so, reason may very well be the source of our moral distinctions. To thwart this argument, Hume's premise must emphasize that our moral distinctions motivate alone. Hume says in support of his second claim, "And this is confirm'd by common experience, which informs us, that men are often govern'd by their duties, and are deter'd from some actions by the opinion of injustice, and impell'd to others by that of obligation" (T 457).

So, if reason alone doesn't motivate, and our making moral distinctions alone does motivate, does it follow, as Hume thinks, that our moral distinctions are not products of reason? I think his conclusion follows, that is, the argument is valid, as do most readers. (This is not to say that all readers agree its premises are true.) The conclusion implies that to call an action morally right or morally wrong, or to judge a person as virtuous or vicious, is not to say anything about the rationality of the actions involved; being vicious is not the same thing as being unreasonable.

People who try to argue that being moral lies in reasoning properly are confusing the beliefs that direct our actions to their ends with the ends themselves. I may judge foolishly in two ways that might lead others to call my actions irrational. (1) I may make a false judgment about the best means to get what I want. For instance, I may take a roundabout and inconvenient route to my destination because I didn't know about a shorter route. (2) I may mistake an object to have a quality I desire, when it actually does not. For instance, I may bite into an apple, believing it to be ripe when it is not. One may say I'm acting irrationally in these two cases, since I might have known better, but this irrationality, Hume says, lies in the judgments about the means to my ends, not in the ends themselves. After all, there is no irrationality in my desiring to get to the hospital quickly or in my craving for an apple. Consequently, when we call behavior irrational, we really mean that it was accompanied by false beliefs, so the behavior technically is not irrational, but the beliefs are. We know, further, that being moral is about one's ends or goals, not about one's beliefs; if it were about the latter, then everyone who had a false belief would be judged as having a vice. But merely having false beliefs does not make a person immoral; morality lies in one's ends (goals), which are set by passions and are not evaluated as rational or irrational (T 459-60).

Morality Not Demonstrated

To offer an even more powerful defense of his thesis that morality does not come from reason alone, Hume considers the two functions of reason with which we are now well-acquainted, demonstration (deduction) and causal reasoning. He considers demonstration first. Clarke, in arguing that morality consists in eternal fitnesses discerned by reason, maintains that morality is a matter of demonstration, of simply knowing how our concepts of things are related to each other, no experience required. So, on this view, morality is defined by relationships; some relations are good and some are bad. Clarke's approach represents the standard moral rationalist line, and Hume's response is to show that something absurd follows from this line. He argues that if morality consisted in relations only, then wherever a bad relation were found in real life, we would have to impute immorality to the situation. If an offspring's killing its parent is unfit in one case, it must be unfit in all others where the same relations hold--namely, where an effect (offspring) destroys its cause (parent). Now, we all agree that a human child murdering a parent is vicious. So, this implies that a sapling produced from an oak tree, when it grows large, will perpetrate immorality if it grows taller than its parent, blocks the parent's light, and causes its death. But this judgment of the tree is absurd. To take another case, consider our judgments of the morality of copulation between siblings. If we call incest immoral in the case of human beings, we must call it so in the case of animals, if relations alone, without facts about the world, are what matter to morality. Again, we have an absurd implication. The rationalist may try to respond that, because animals lack the reason necessary to know right from wrong, we don't apply morality to animal behavior (nor to tree behavior). But then the rationalist would be admitting that the criterion of morality depends on something besides the relations involved. So, Hume concludes, morality does not come from deductive reasoning, which deals with relations of ideas (T 466-68).

Morality Not From Causal Reasoning: "Is" and "Ought"

Might morality come from reason in its second function, namely, causal reasoning? Causal reasoning gives us beliefs in matters of fact, beliefs that represent to us the way things are in the world. Do our moral distinctions lie in beliefs about the way the world is? Well, Hume asks, in what fact would morality lie? He has us consider an action and ask ourselves this question. Take a case of deliberate murder, and list all the facts about it that you know. You know that it was premeditated and done out of malice. You know that it was committed with a knife at 11:45 p.m. on a Thursday. You know that the victim felt the pain of the wounds and bled to death. Hume says, "The vice entirely escapes you as long as you consider the object." But you also know that you find the act despicable:

> You can never find it [the vice] till you turn your reflexion into your own breast, and find a sentiment of disapprobation, which arises in you, towards this action. Here is a matter of fact, but 'tis and object of feeling, not of reason. It lies in yourself not in the object (T 468-69).

Hume is arguing here that compiling facts about an action or a person does not by itself give us a moral evaluation; that evaluation comes in responding to those facts, and it only comes when we react to the information in a certain way. We experience a feeling of disapproval, an uncomfortable emotion, when we observe certain actions, like the

68

murder; we find in ourselves a feeling of approval, a sort of pleasure, when we observe other actions, like someone helping the victim. But if no one ever reacted emotionally to actions or actors, no one would make moral judgments; they would just contemplate facts.

Hume's point is that sentiment or emotion or passion is at the foundation of our moral distinctions. Those who attempt to reason to a conclusion about morality based on facts are making a logical mistake. Consider the argument: (1) The murderer acted out of malice; (2) The victim died a painful death; (3) Therefore, the murder was a vicious act. This is not a valid argument; the conclusion does not follow from the premises, and adding more facts about the murder to the case will not help. In order to get to the judgment in (3), we must supply a claim about virtue and vice, or about how judgments of virtue and vice are made. Consider: (1) The murderer acted out of malice; (2) The victim died a painful death; (3) Purposely causing unnecessary pain is vicious; (4) Therefore, the murder was a vicious act. Now, the conclusion follows, because we have a claim about viciousness that connects the conclusion to the premises (and we know that acting out of malice implies the pain inflicted was unnecessary). From where does (3), the added premise, that causing unnecessary pain is vicious, itself come? It doesn't come from considering facts alone, not even the fact that people don't like pain. Hume argues that it can only come from appealing to our emotional reactions to cases of inflicting pain unnecessarily. When we react with disapproval or abhorrence of actions that inflict pain, then we find ourselves applying a moral evaluation to those actions.

Hume is famous for his dictum that no "ought" follows from an "is," which is to say that no factual statements by themselves support a conclusion about value, about what we ought to do. The premises of an argument with an "ought" conclusion must always have a value statement among them. But that statement must itself be based on something ultimately; it can't be based on other value statements to infinity. Hume's answer is that the value statements come from our sentiments, our emotional reactions to actions and persons performing them. What is the nature of these moral sentiments?

Sentiment, Sympathy, and Natural Virtue

If our moral distinctions cannot derive from reason (from our ideas), they must come from the non-rational, perceiving part of our nature (from our impressions). This conclusion leads Hume at one point to say that our moral distinctions come from a moral "sense," as though our emotional reactions to characters and actions are perceptions of their moral qualities, just as our color and taste reactions, etc., are perceptions of objects' physical qualities. Of course, when we perceive the colors and tastes of objects, we need have no concept of the things to which we are reacting; we don't have to know what an object is in order to perceive its color. But when we react to actions and characters, we are reacting to our concepts of these. If I don't know what the figures, shapes, colors, and sounds before me are--that they are, for instance, a case of one person lying to another out of self-interest--I won't react in a way that indicates to me anything about the morality of the situation. Hence, moral sensation requires that I conceptualize the object of perception. We shouldn't, however, emphasize the analogy between moral and physical perception too much, since the analogy is not perfect, and the implications it may have for our moral judgments are not always consistent with what Hume actually says about them. Instead, we should follow the details of Hume's actual account.

Hume explains that the feelings upon which our moral distinctions depend are feelings of approval and disapproval. The characters we approve, we consider virtuous; and those we disapprove, vicious. We may at first think that approval and disapproval are not feelings at all, but rather reflective judgments for which we offer reasons: Your mom disapproves of your lifestyle or of your boyfriend (or girlfriend), and these are judgments she makes of the quality of your life based on her concept of what counts as a good life or a good relationship. But Hume would say that our looking at approval or disapproval in this way is confused; the factors that seem like reasons for your mom's assessment are causes of her feelings. Your mother feels an attitude of disapproval *first*, and her assessment of your life or relationship depends on that attitude (some readers of Hume would say it is identical to that attitude). The mental states of approval and disapproval are versions of pleasure and pain, on Hume's theory; after all, to approve of something is to feel satisfaction from it, and to disapprove is to feel dissatisfaction. The former is pleasant and the latter painful. Hume writes,

> An action, or sentiment, or character is virtuous or vicious; why? because its view causes a pleasure or uneasiness of a particular kind. In giving a reason for the pleasure or uneasiness, we sufficiently explain the vice or virtue. To have the sense of virtue, is nothing but to *feel* a satisfaction of a particular kind from the contemplation of a character. The very *feeling* constitutes our praise or admiration (T 471).

So far, Hume has been trying to describe the origin of our moral judgments. If his theory is correct, it will have to account for some obvious facts about the way we make our moral distinctions. We know that we don't make a moral evaluation every time we have a feeling of approval, admiration, or pleasure (or the opposite). A new kitchen knife that pleases is surely not virtuous, and neither is a pleasurable glass of wine. And we also know that our moral judgments don't always track with our feelings of approval and disapproval, even when they are about persons; I may feel only mild disapproval of my own child's behavior while others find it obnoxious. Are there some general principles about our feelings, our judgments, or our natures that Hume might site to explain these features of our moral distinctions?

He can easily answer the problem of approving of inanimate objects by calling on principles he has earlier explained. We have already noted in the theory of the indirect passions that the objects of pride, humility, love, and hatred are always persons--another or myself. Virtue and vice, Hume argues, are among the causes of these passions: They are features of a person's character that inspire feelings of pleasure or pain. The answer to the second problem, why our moral distinctions, on the one hand, and our feelings of approval and disapproval, on the other, do not always correspond, requires an explanation Hume has not yet appealed to.

Sympathy and the General Point of View

In the attempt to explain our mental life in terms of a few natural principles, Hume finds that a fundamental human principle, sympathy, underlies our moral judgments. Why do we feel pleasure at the thought of some actions or characters, and pain at the thought of others? Hume's answer is that it is natural for us to sympathize with the feelings of others. Sympathy is the capacity to turn the idea of the passions of another into an impression of our own (T 317). We infer the feelings of others from their behavior; this idea of their feelings takes on a greater force and vivacity as we imagine ourselves affected by the circumstances of others' situations. I drive by the scene of a terrible car accident, and I cringe at the thought of the bodies in the twisted wreckage; the thought of their suffering causes me pain (not physical, but mental, pain). When I think about a heinous murderer like Hitler or Pol Pot, the explanation of my disapproval, which is a form of pain, is that I sympathize with the victims of the murderer's actions, and I know

71

that the victims suffered greatly. My approval of the acts of a generous person like Mother Teresa, who worked for the poor in Calcutta, is a result of my sympathy with those whose lives she made better.

But we don't sympathize to the same extent with all human beings because the principles of mental association Hume has earlier detailed also influence sympathy. I sympathize to a greater degree with those who are related to me by contiguity, resemblance, or causality. I feel worse about the diagnosis of my neighbor's illness than I do about the stranger I read about in the paper with the same disease; this is because I am close to my neighbor, in physical and psychological contiguity. We are more affected by the feelings of those with whom we find something in common than by the feelings of those with whom we share little, because the resemblances between us makes it easier to imagine the others' feelings. And I take greater pleasure in my daughter's accomplishments than I do in that of an acquaintance's child because of ties of causality (T 318). But if such sympathetic feelings are the foundation of our moral judgments, does it follow that, even though my child has the same traits as another, I think the former more virtuous than the latter because my feelings of approval are stronger? Of course not. Hume says, "nor can I feel the same lively pleasure from the virtues of a person, who liv'd in *Greece* two thousand years ago, that I feel from the virtues of a familiar friend and acquaintance. Yet I do not say, that I esteem one more than the other: . . ."(T 581). So, now we are back to the problem how sentiments can be the source of our moral distinctions when the former often vary in cases where the latter don't. Hume's answer is this:

> . . . every particular man has a peculiar position with regard to others; and 'tis impossible we cou'd ever converse together on any reasonable terms, were each of us to consider characters and persons, only as they appear from his peculiar point of view. In order, therefore, to prevent those continual *contradictions*, and arrive at a more *stable* judgment of things, we fix on some *steady* and *general* points of view; and always, in our thoughts, place ourselves in them, whatever may be our present situation (T 581-82).

In other words, in order to communicate about morality and avoid practical problems arising from conflicting moral judgments, we consider our sympathetic feelings indicative of moral distinctions *only* when we take up a generally shared perspective on an action or character. In so doing, we consider the effects of an action or character in isolation from our personal connections to the actor. More specifically, the general point of view from which we make moral distinctions is the viewpoint of one who sympathizes with the circle of people most directly affected by the agent's actions. To sympathize with this "inner circle," the spectator's feelings must mirror the feelings of those who are the direct recipients of the agent's actions and their consequences. For instance, when I make a moral judgment about a dictator in a distant country, I think about the effects on the citizens there and identify with their feelings; I try to do it in the same way I think about and respond to the effects of my local government on citizens here. In each case, I identify only with the feelings of people directly affected by the government actions. To use another case, when I consider the behavior of my child from a moral perspective, I imagine myself affected by her actions in the way others around her are and consider my feelings in that state of mind, rather than my feelings in my role as mother, indicative of virtue and vice.

Hume refers to taking up the general point of view as a kind of correction of our sentiments. He remarks,

> Such corrections are common with regard to all the senses; and indeed t'were impossible we cou'd ever make use of language, or communicate our sentiments to one another, did we not correct the momentary appearances of things, and over look our present situation (T 582).

We don't pronounce on the size or shape or color of something under just any circumstances. The Empire State Building looks small at a distance and very tall on close approach; my shoes look black under the lighting in this room and blue in the sunlight. A discussion of the height of the Empire State Building in a book on architecture would be baffling if we had no agreed standards of measuring such things; if we attended to all perspectives equally, we couldn't say much of anything about its size. Is it taller or smaller than the Eiffel Tower? Is it taller or smaller than an automobile? We correct the "momentary appearances of things" and set a standard perspective for judging the qualities of objects, so that our terms and social interactions make sense. Likewise, on Hume's view, the moral life would not make sense, did we not have a general point of view from which to specify our moral distinctions.

One might ask of Hume's account: What happens if I try to take up the general point of view, try to sympathize with the circle of those affected directly by an agent, but I can't really get my feelings to change, because the people involved are just so distant? In other words,

I know what feelings I would have if I were really in the general point of view, but I simply can't push myself to feel as intensely about strangers as I do about my family and friends, or to lessen the intensity of the feelings I have about my family and friends to match my feelings about strangers in a similar situation. Hume acknowledges that this is also natural, and he responds: "Experience soon teaches us this method of correcting our sentiments, or at least, of correcting our language, where the sentiments are more stubborn and inalterable" (T 582). Hence, if we realize how we would feel if we successfully achieved the general point of view, this is sufficient for us to express the proper judgments. We can conform our way of speaking about morality to the feelings we would have in the "moral" point of view and avoid the problems of talking at cross-purposes.

Natural Virtue

The moral theory we have so far seen in Hume is an account of the origin of our moral distinctions. It is intended to describe how we make those distinctions and from what principles in human nature they come. He has said nothing yet about what character traits are actually virtuous or vicious, except insofar as he uses examples, but his account does have implications for the content of morality as well. Hume's is a spectator theory of the virtues. In other words, the content of morality-- which traits are virtues and which are vices--is determined by the reactions of a spectator who has taken up the general point of view. A character trait is virtuous if an observer approves, through sympathy, of the effects of that trait on others from the common perspective; a character trait is a vice if such an observer disapproves. For a motive to be considered part of character, it must be a motive that operates consistently over time in a person to produce action. We cannot observe the motives of others, but their behavior and its effects are open to view. We take certain behavior as indicative of kindness and certain behavior as indicative of envy, and so forth. Since we know from experience the effects of these various behaviors, we can determine from the spectator perspective which motives are virtues and which are vices, whether anyone at present possesses them.

Hume says that we will find a natural division among the approved features, the virtues. One class consists of those that make a person able to promote his or her own interests; the other consists of those that make a person fit for society. In other words, the virtues are described as those traits that make us useful and agreeable to ourselves, and those that make us useful and agreeable to others. Hume spends a good deal of time in the *Enquiry Concerning the Principles of Morals*, his more popular presentation of his ethics, discussing these different categories of virtues and vices. Of qualities useful to the self, he says,

> Besides *discretion, caution, enterprise, industry, assiduity, frugality, economy, good-sense, prudence, discernment*; besides these endowments, I say, whose very names force an avowal of their merit, there are many others, to which the most determined scepticism cannot for a moment refuse the tribute of praise and approbation. *Temperance, sobriety, patience, constancy, perseverance, forethought, considerateness, secrecy, order, insinuation, address, presence of mind, quickness of conception, facility of expression*; these, and a thousand more of the same kind, no man will ever deny to be excellencies and perfections (EPM 242-43).

Among the qualities immediately agreeable to ourselves are cheerfulness, tranquility, and serenity. Qualities useful to society include generosity, gratitude, kindness, and courage; qualities immediately agreeable to others are politeness, wit, ingenuity, modesty, decency, and cleanliness. Hume calls such features of character "natural" virtue because in every instance they give us, as spectators, pleasure through natural sympathy.

A notable circumstance of human nature that emerges from Hume's study of the way we make moral distinctions is the mind's tendency to rely upon "general rules." We saw prominently in Hume's discussion of causality that the mind passes from an impression to an idea because of a habit of association. This tendency is at work in morality as well. We take actions as signs of character; we assume the general point of view as the perspective from which we make moral judgments, rather than relying on our "unregulated" sympathies; and when actions do not produce their typical consequences, we pronounce on a character according to the effects those actions would normally have. One's bungled attempt to save a person from the path of an oncoming car is still a sign of that person's goodness, despite the bad results. Hume puts it well:

> Where a person is possess'd of a character, that in its natural tendency is beneficial to society, we esteem him virtuous, and are delighted with the view of his character, even tho' particular accidents prevent its operation, and incapacitate him from being

75

serviceable to his friends and country. Virtue in rags is still virtue;
. . . .

    . . . Where a character is, in every respect, fitted to be beneficial to society, the imagination passes easily from the cause to the effect, without considering that there are still some circumstances wanting to render the cause a compleat one. (T 584-85).

Some Comments on Hume's Theory of Natural Virtue

    Hume's theory of natural virtue raises several questions of debate for readers, some questions that Hume himself does not address directly. It is worth considering a couple of them briefly.

    (1) It looks as though the main goal of Hume's theory is to describe our practice of evaluating others, rather than to articulate any norms that are to guide our behavior. If this is so, then his theory lacks a key feature we want in a plausible moral theory--an account of what we *ought* to do! But Hume has some things to say in reply to this protest. His theory is not only about judging others, since we can also turn our moral sensibility on our own character. Hume says that when we discover virtuous traits that others generally possess and that we lack, we have an unpleasant feeling toward ourselves[2], which prompts us to change our ordinary behavior. He calls this feeling "the sense of duty." The sense of duty is an awareness that we lack virtue, the traits others find pleasing, and it motivates us to do the actions a virtuous person would do. So, I may be motivated by my sense of duty to tell the truth because I'm uneasy about my dishonest inclinations (T 479).

    While Hume's theory is foremost a virtue ethics--the morally best people are motivated by their natural virtues--he also has an account of how a person lacking virtue might be motivated to do the right thing. After all, one of the crucial claims in Hume's argument against the moral rationalists is the claim that morality motivates; that claim means that our awareness of what is virtuous and what is vicious has an influence on our motivations. The sense of duty explains how this is so. While this reply does not entirely acquit Hume's theory on the charge that it lacks an account of "oughts," it does show that he has pinpointed a mechanism in human behavior that accounts for our getting direction or guidance from our moral distinctions and from our nature.

    (2) Does Hume's view that moral distinctions cannot be based on reason alone imply that there are simply no beliefs about morality?

Hume has argued that reason gives us beliefs, and when he argues that reason by itself doesn't motivate, he is arguing that beliefs, which represent the way the world is, don't influence actions by themselves. Representative (cognitive) states don't motivate. We know he has also argued that, for this reason, morality, which does motivate, ultimately depends on feeling. But does this mean, then, that when we make a pronouncement, such as, "Benevolence is a virtue," we are not stating a thought with a cognitive content, but, rather, expressing a feeling? To express a feeling is to say nothing, but to signify how we feel, in the way that laughing or crying shows whether we are happy or sad. Furthermore, if we were saying something about the world when we make moral pronouncements, what would we be saying? That benevolence is a virtue or malice is a vice doesn't seem to say anything about how things are, but about how they ought to be.

Such reasoning has led many philosophers to conclude that Hume's theory implies that there simply are no moral beliefs, that the practice of morality is solely a matter of having feelings, expressing them, and being motivated by them (a view called "non-cognitivism"). But the case for this understanding of Hume is not so clear-cut. Remember, when Hume argues that morality is a matter of feeling, he has us look inside ourselves, and here we find "a matter of fact," but one, which is not discoverable by reason. Instead, it is discovered by sentiment, because it is a fact about how we feel when we make a moral pronouncement. After all, no one has to infer by reasoning how he or she feels. So, here Hume doesn't seem to deny that there is some kind of facts that gives morality content; rather, he implies that, whatever these facts consist in, they are not like our causal beliefs--attributions of properties to objects in the world. Of course, there is much more to be said about the issue, and the discussion over whether Hume's view is non-cognitivist (and over the merits of non-cognitivism) continues.[3]

Justice, or Artificial Virtue

The practice of morality includes more than our distinguishing between traits like generosity and stinginess, gratitude and ingratitude, kindness and cruelty. Morality also includes our using notions of the just and the unjust. These notions are different from the others because acts of justice are ones we approve, not because they are the immediate sources of pleasure to those directly affected by the actor, but because we derive a kind of pleasure from the system in which they play a part.

For instance, if a poor person borrows money from an uncharitable miser and doesn't repay the loan, that person is actually better off, and the miser no worse off. A moral spectator would naturally take pleasure in a situation where a poor person is benefited and the miser isn't hurt. And yet, we want to say that justice requires that all loans be repaid, no matter who the debtor and who the lender. How can a sentiment be the ground of this judgment, if natural sentiment runs contrary to it? This is the paradox Hume intends to explain with his theory of artificial virtue.

The First Virtuous Motive

When we approve of an action, we always take ourselves to be approving of the motive from which the action originates. A good character consists of virtuous motives. Now, some philosophers have argued that what characterizes a virtuous motive is that it is a regard for moral duty. In other words, on their view, virtuous people are those who are motivated by a concern for doing the right thing. This means that people are not good for being kind or grateful or generous, but for caring about doing moral actions, for being prompted by what Hume has called the sense of duty. If this is so, then there is an answer to the question what makes an act like repaying a loan to a miser a good thing, even though we don't naturally approve of it: The act is right because it is done with regard to the virtue, or the honesty, of the action. Regard for morality, on this view, is the motive that makes the act moral. But Hume argues that this view makes no sense.

Hume's argument is that, for an action to be virtuous, it has to be done from a virtuous motive. For instance, my giving to charity is virtuous if I act out of generosity, but not if I act out of the desire to get the praise of others (a version of self-interest). If we try to define a virtuous motive in terms of the virtue of the action it produces (rather than in terms of our approval of a trait), and the virtue of the act depends on the virtue of its motive, we reason in a circle. For instance, consider what happens when I apply the rule, "An act is virtuous because it is done with respect to the virtue of the action," to the example of my repaying a loan. Why is it virtuous for me to repay this loan? The answer is that it is virtuous for me to repay the loan because I am moved by the thought that repaying loans is virtuous. Nothing here tells me *why* repaying a loan is virtuous. Hume says we have to find "the first virtuous motive," a natural motive of which we approve and which bestows value on the action. Then we will have an account of why the action is virtuous (T 478-80).

78

The Origin of Property and Justice

Hume's theory of justice is geared to answer two questions: (1) From what motive are the rules of justice established? (2) Why do we consider observance of these rules virtuous, and violation of them vicious?

(1) Hume observes that people in nature, without an established society to structure their behavior, would be at a great disadvantage. Each person, on his or her own, would have a difficult time providing food, shelter, clothing, and the amenities that make life worth living. Furthermore, our natural emotions can interfere with our living well. Since we are inclined to care about ourselves and those close to us and want to provide the external goods that fulfill their and our own desires and necessities, there exists an instability among people. If there is a scarcity of the resources needed to fulfill these desires, then possessions are never secure. It is a familiar story of the state of nature, articulated in various forms by other political philosophers.

The remedy to this situation comes from an artifice, or an artificial structure, which humans create to make their possessions stable and secure. They establish by a convention or an agreement a set of rules by which they regulate their actions. Hume emphasizes that the agreement into which people enter is not a promise, since promise-making itself is only intelligible after the conventions which are being set forth with this act are established. (Promises require more than an expression of intention on the part of the promiser; they also need recognition on the part of others that these words establish an obligation.) Hume says that the agreement which establishes the rules of justice is analogous to the situation of two men rowing a boat: "Two men, who pull the oars of a boat, do it by an agreement or convention, tho' they have never given promises to each other" (T 490). The rowing is done by the one on the supposition that the other will do the same. The conventions for the stability of possessions do not arise suddenly, but gradually and through trial and error, Hume says. So, there is good reason for thinking this agreement is not a contract, but a natural evolution of practice.

From what motive do the conventions for respecting property, the heart of justice, come? Hume's answer is that it can only be from self-interest. Might we have been motivated by an extensive benevolent affection for all of mankind to respect their possessions? First, we possess no such extensive benevolence. Second, the proposal makes no sense: If we naturally pursued the public interest, we wouldn't need to establish the conventions in the first place. But how is it that self-interest can motivate the establishment of justice, when it's also the case that each of us is not personally advantaged by every act dictated by the system of justice? I am, after all, better off if I take something you have that I need than if I respect your right to your property. Of course, the answer is that, while single acts are not always conducive to a particular individual's interest, the whole scheme is to the benefit of each. "And even every individual must find himself a gainer, on ballancing the account; since without justice, society must immediately dissolve, and every one must fall into that savage and solitary condition . . . " (T 497). So, Hume has answered the first question about justice: It is derived from the motive of self-interest. This is the natural motive for which he was looking.

(2) Why do we consider compliance with the rules of justice virtuous, and violation of them vicious? The answer is the same one Hume gave for the natural virtues: We approve of one and disapprove of the other. Our approval and disapproval in this context is not based on self-interest, but is moral approval and disapproval--rooted in sympathy with others when we take up the general point of view. But this means we are capable of an even broader point of view than what Hume describes as the source of natural virtue, since it overcomes the problem of our approving unjust actions that benefit certain individuals. We come to see an unjust action as a perpetration "prejudicial to human society" and "pernicious to every one that approaches the person guilty of it" (T 499). Furthermore, we not only disapprove of others who violate the rules of justice, but we sympathize with the disapproving sentiments of others toward our own unjust behavior as well. So Hume concludes that a sympathy with the public interest is the source of the moral distinctions we apply to ourselves under the system of justice.

In view of the problem with which Hume began his discussion of justice, one might very well ask: If we lack benevolence extensive enough to care naturally about the possessions of others, then why do we have sympathy extensive enough to identify with society under the rules of justice? Hume sees sympathy as capable of cultivation in a way that can make its purview broader than that of benevolence. Hume believes us capable of transforming our narrower sympathies by reflection on the advantages of the system of justice in such a way that we approve of actions that obey the societal rules even when they distress those most directly affected by an agent's acts (as in the repaying of the loan to a miser). Some readers nonetheless think that how this psychological change happens in us is not so clear in Hume's account. Do we somehow sympathize with projected benefits and advantages that accrue to persons under the system as a whole?

80

Conclusion

If the account of justice works, then sympathy must be transformed beyond the capacity to take on the pleasures and pains of the agent's close circle into the capacity to feel approval at actions that serve the long-term good of all persons in society. Whether or not Hume's account has difficulties, it is notable that both here and in his discussion of the natural virtues, he offers a constructive, naturalistic account; Hume is not skeptical about the practice of morality. Any doubts about the external world and the self are left behind because, no matter the philosophical implications of Humean epistemology, we find ourselves faced with the art of living and join in the practice of morality.

Discussion Questions

1. What does Hume mean by saying that no "ought" follows from an "is"?
2. Hume says that we only make moral judgments by regard to our sympathetic feelings when we have assumed a general point of view, which eliminates the influence of personal connections. He also says that sometimes our feelings are stubborn, and so we make moral judgments that conform to the feelings we would have, were we able to achieve the proper viewpoint. But if I have to infer how I *would* feel, does this make morality dependent on reason in a crucial way after all? (A hard question!)
3. Explain the problem in holding that a regard for morality or justice is the motive that makes actions virtuous.

Endnotes

1. Published in 1706 as *A Discourse concerning the Unchangeable Obligations of Natural Religion.*
2. He calls it a feeling of self-hatred, but we have seen in his discussion of the passions that the object of hatred is always another person. I would argue that it's a feeling of self-disapproval.
3. For a non-cognitivist reading of Hume, see J.L. Mackie, *Hume's Moral Theory* (London; Boston: Routledge & Kegan Paul, 1980).

81

6

Religious Belief

Hume was critical of religious belief, and especially of the doctrines of organized religion. He was no doubt influenced by the atrocities committed by the Church in centuries previous to his. In his essay on moral practices, "A Dialogue," appended to his *Enquiry Concerning the Principles of Morals*, he refers to those who lead "artificial lives." Reason and human nature do not govern their behavior, but instead they allow religion to replace the role of philosophy; religion prescribes to them universal rules, governed by a system of infinite and distant reward and punishment. "They are in a different element from the rest of mankind; and the natural principles of their mind play not with the same regularity, ..."[1] But Hume's critique of religion is not merely an emotional response to events and people in his culture; he has arguments, framed by empiricism, for his views. His critique of religion is a practical application of the principles of human nature he has discovered, and his work may partly be seen as an attempt to replace the appeal to God's authority prominent in moral theory of his day with the human mechanism of sympathy. His views are revealed in great detail in his posthumously published, *Dialogues Concerning Natural Religion*. But two sections at the end of his first *Enquiry*, which treat miracles and the afterlife, provoked great backlash during his lifetime.

Miracles

The majority of believers in miracles do not claim to have witnessed them; rather, they take the occurrence of miracles to be fact based on the testimony of other people. Accordingly, Hume's discussion of the legitimacy of belief in miracles, offered in the first *Enquiry*, focuses on the value of human testimony as good evidence.

We know that each of our beliefs in a matter of fact is based on an experience of a constant conjunction of events, but some conjunctions are more constant than others. It would be irrational to assert with certainty that the third week of July will be warmer than the first week of October, since temperatures vary within months, and our generalizations about them are not so secure. We consider beliefs as more or less probable, depending on the evidence, and the wise person judges probable those beliefs, which on balance, are supported by the greater number of observations. Although Hume's philosophy shows us that we could always be mistaken, claims based on an exceptionless constant conjunction of events we believe with the greatest assurance. These, Hume says, we regard as "proven." So, we take as proven that snow is cold or that ordinary paper burns. We've never experienced conjunctions to the contrary that diminish our degree of conviction.

Human testimony or eyewitness report is one form of evidence on which we often rely. Before we consider "proven," or even probable, the content of the belief to which someone testifies, we examine the possible counterevidence. Accordingly, we explore whether the witnesses are credible; whether there are witnesses with contradictory testimony; whether we know of conjunctions of events that lead to beliefs contrary to that of this testimonial; and so forth.

Now, Hume asks, what is a miracle?

> A miracle is a violation of the laws of nature; . . . . It is no miracle that a man, seemingly in good health, should die on a sudden; because such a kind of death, though more unusual than any other, has yet been frequently observed to happen. But it is a miracle that a dead man should come to life; because that has never before been observed in any age or country. There must, therefore, be a uniform experience against every miraculous event, otherwise the event would not merit that appellation (EHU 114-15).

Given this characterization, Hume argues that a testimony is only sufficient to command belief in a miracle, if the falsehood of the testimony would be even more miraculous than the miracle itself. In other words, we weigh the experience contrary to a belief in the event against the experience in favor of the witness and his or her testimonial. If it is more incredible that the witness be wrong than that the event occurred, we accept the belief in the miraculous event. But, was there ever a case of the miraculous that answers to this criterion? Was there ever a testimony that amounted to a proof? And could there be? Hume offers four observations in support of a negative answer.

First, there simply are no people who hold such a high degree of credibility, integrity, and education as to be beyond suspicion and doubt. Who among us would believe someone--anyone--who tells a story that runs contrary to all of our sense experience, simply on the basis of that person's word?

Second, certainly there are persons who do believe in miracles based on testimony, but their beliefs are not based entirely on that testimony. Rather, they are persuaded in part by the wonder of the events being described, for it is a fact about us that the passions of surprise and wonder, which are pleasant emotions, incline us toward belief in the events from which these emotions arise. In his analysis of belief, Hume discussed the effect of the passions on belief--remember, for instance, how fearful people tend to believe more readily in the presence of danger. Here we have another example of this principle at work in human nature. How many people are inclined to believe in the existence of UFO's or in mental telepathy or in psychics who foretell the future, because the prospect of such wonders is fascinating or exciting? The effect of such a disposition is multiplied, Hume says, by the fact that the "spirit of religion" cooperates with the love of wonder to produce belief in the miraculous and the supernatural.

Third, Hume argues that it is a presumption against beliefs in the miraculous that they originated in ignorant and remote civilizations. About this observation we might be skeptical, and his examples seem insufficient to establish his point for contemporary readers, so I will not discuss it further. His fourth observation is more persuasive. Hume claims that there is no testimony for the miraculous "that is not opposed by an infinite number of witnesses; so that not only the miracle destroys the credit of the testimony, but the testimony destroys itself" (EHU 121). What can he mean? His point is that the various religious sects that offer testimony for miracles aim to be mutually exclusive and suppose that belief in their miracles constitutes belief in their system. So, the effect of a testimonial from a Chinese believer, with a religion distinct from a Roman believer, is to undercut the testimonial of the Roman believer; but the testimonial of the latter has the same effect on the former. So, because of religious factions and the identity of miracles with an exclusive sect, Hume thinks that religious testimonials undermine their own purposes.

Regardless of the strength of the considerations Hume cites in support of his view, there is one line of thought he might have pursued that follows nicely from his analysis of causality. Miracles are part of religious belief because they are seen as actions of a Supreme Being. Given that all attributions of causality require previous experiences of a certain kind of event followed by another kind of event, Hume might have asked how we could ever know that anything in particular was the cause of these random events we call miracles. By definition, they cannot fit into the regularities that allow us to identify causes. Assuming that such events occur, they appear random; yet we attribute them to the power of God--but on what basis? We have no grounds upon which to attribute them to anything in particular.

The Existence and Nature of God

Hume's *Dialogues Concerning Natural Religion* focus on issues that arise within the area of natural, as opposed to revealed, theology. Revealed theology consists of religious doctrine that comes to human beings through revelation, or supernatural means--inspired scriptures, God's talking directly to select individuals, etc. Natural theology deals with religious beliefs that are susceptible to "proofs" based on information accessible by the natural faculties--arguments built on reasoning from sensory data. The dialogues depict a conversation among three characters, who each represent a different perspective on the existence and nature of God. Demea and Cleanthes are religious believers. Cleanthes represents the scientific believer, who, like Newton, wants to use observations about nature and scientific investigation to draw conclusions about God's attributes. Demea is the more typical believer, who thinks that what we can know about God comes only through reason and authority. Philo is the non-believer and skeptic, who tries to point out the fallacies in Cleanthes's arguments.

It may seem obvious that Philo is Hume's mouthpiece, yet it has been intriguing to Hume's readers that, toward the end of the *Dialogues,* Philo declares that skepticism leads to Christian belief. Furthermore, the fourth character, the young Pamphilus, who is a spectator and pupil to the discussion, declares in the final paragraph that the views of Cleanthes, the scientific believer, approach closest to the truth. In his "Natural History of Religion" and in the mouth of Philo in the *Dialogues*, Hume also avers that reasonable people, contrasted with the superstitious, silly believer, cannot help but posit a designer behind the order they find in the universe. These puzzling turns in the conversation of the *Dialogues* and Hume's remarks elsewhere have led readers to debate Hume's real views on religious belief: Might he have been a deist (one who believes in a non-personal God, who has no interactions with creation), or an agnostic, rather than an atheist?

The conversation in the *Dialogues* focuses chiefly on an argument from analogy for the attributes of the Supreme Being. Arguments from analogy draw a conclusion about the features of something based on its similarities to another thing about which more is known. How strong any particular argument from analogy is depends on how many features two objects of comparison have in common and how relevant those features are to the characteristics attributed to the second object in the conclusion. For instance, here is an unsound argument: Because your new automobile has the same color and the same kind of interior upholstery as my car, and my car is reliable, then yours will be. Obviously, color and upholstery are irrelevant to a car's reliability; it is more pertinent to cite similarities in manufacturers and engine design. In the *Dialogues*, Cleanthes offers an argument about God, which goes:

> Look round the world: Contemplate the whole and every part of it: You will find it to be nothing but one great machine, subdivided into an infinite number of lesser machines, which again admit of subdivisions to a degree beyond what human senses and faculties can trace and explain . . . .The curious adapting of means to ends, throughout all nature, resembles exactly, though it much exceeds, the productions of human contrivance; of human design, thought, wisdom, and intelligence. Since therefore the effects resemble each other, we are led to infer, by all the rules of analogy, that the causes also resemble, and that the Author of Nature is somewhat similar to the mind of man, though possessed of much larger faculties, proportioned to the grandeur of the work which he has executed (DNR 15).

So, Cleanthes sees the analogy between the workings of nature and the workings of a human-made production, such as a house or a computer, as proof of the existence and intelligence of Deity.

Philo, the skeptic, remarks that reasonable people will not disagree over the existence of Deity, given that we have to believe every event must have a cause, including the beginning of the universe. But his criticisms of Cleanthes's argument are two. First, it is impossible for us to understand the attributes of God. All of our ideas depend on and are limited by our experiences; to speculate about the characteristics of a divine being goes beyond the limits of our experience, and so we couldn't have an idea of what we're talking about. Second, Philo thinks the analogy upon which the argument turns is weak. When we reason from numerous instances of experiencing smoke with fire that the two will occur together in the future, we are on firm footing, because fire is always similar in all respects to past instances of fire. But the resemblance between the whole universe and a human artifact, like a house, is very slight. What do they have in common?

Cleanthes attempts a rebuttal, pointing major similarities between the two. He notes that the parts of a house are designed in such a way as to fulfill certain purposes--for instance, the steps of a stairway are of a certain size and proportion so as to accommodate the climbing of human legs. But Philo cannot agree in general with the attempt to use a comparison between a part of nature and the whole of nature to draw any conclusion. What can be said of a part does not necessarily apply to the whole: Can we know about a tree from the motion of one of its leaves? And the parts we do know are small in number compared to all the parts of the universe as a whole. Just because brick, stone, iron, wood, and brass do not at this time in our part of the universe arrange themselves into a functional order without a designer is no good reason to suppose the same was true of the whole at the beginning of time. What we say of a mature universe, just as what we say of a mature human, does not necessarily apply to the thing in its embryonic state.

The conversation turns more specifically to the attributes of God, and Cleanthes attempts a comparison of God's mind to the human mind: As we can discern the mind and intentions of an author from her book, so too, we can discover God's attributes from creation. But Demea, the orthodox believer, is offended by comparing God to mere humans and maintains that God's intellect must be different from the human mind, which is populated with all sorts of sentiments--gratitude, envy, love, resentment. Sentiments are changeable, but God is not. God is by definition perfect and immutable, but also unknowable. Cleanthes, however, sees such a position as little different from atheism or skepticism, since such positions, too, assert the incomprehensibility of a first cause. Furthermore, Cleanthes cannot see how a mind without changing feelings and ideas could have any thought or reason at all.

Philo points out that Cleanthes's view, which attributes changing ideas to the mind of God, needs to appeal to some explanation of the new ideas that come into God's mind--why do they come in the order in which they do? Why is one idea followed by another? (This is a question with which we're quite familiar in Hume's own theory of ideas.) Philo thinks such an explanation must either result in appealing to an infinite chain of causes, or else stop with something like an appeal to "the rational faculty:" It happens this way because it is just the way

87

rationality is. But the latter sounds nothing like the personal God Cleanthes wants to defend! Cleanthes thinks there is no reason to worry about the cause of the ideas in God's mind, since this is like asking for the cause of the cause. God is simply the cause of God's ideas.

Philo wants to explore Cleanthes's "anthropomorphic" view of God, that is, he wants to find out what follows from seeing God as human-like, in the way Cleanthes does. As one might expect, such a view, since it implies lack of perfection in the Deity, gets Cleanthes in all kinds of trouble when it comes to a comparison with more orthodox conceptions of God. First, if God is fallible, there is no reason to think that the present universe was the product of a first attempt. Just as a bumbling carpenter might finally produce a beautiful ship at the end of much trial and error, so too, God might have botched many tries at producing this creation. Second, since God is not necessarily unity and perfection, we have no reason to suppose that there is only one God; the universe may be the result of a committee of creators. Third, we might as well think of Deity as possessing a body or as reproducing, just like all other things in nature with which we are familiar. But who, among religious believers, can rest content with these allegations? Cleanthes, too, wants to deny them, but he seems to have no ground.

The conversation also turns to the issue whether other analogies are more apt to describe the universe than that to a machine. Is the universe more like an animal or a vegetable? If it were more like either, then its cause would lie in something like generation or reproduction. Plants and animals reproduce without the intervention of designers; they have the seeds of reproduction within themselves. Philo and Cleanthes debate the question whether the universe might be self-generating in this way. What is most interesting in their discussion is that each takes the implication of the analogy to animals and vegetation differently. Cleanthes argues that if the universe is like a plant or an animal, then it arose from generation, but the principle of generation implies a rational design and designer! Philo argues that if there is design in the universe similar to the design in plants and animals, it indicates that the universe arose from a principle of generation, period.

The last significant topic Hume's interlocutors address is the problem of evil. The problem of evil constitutes a long-standing objection to the existence of the traditional God of Christianity. Traditional Christianity asserts that God is all-powerful and all-good. The problem is that it is an obvious fact that there are bad things in the world: physical and mental pain; immoralities committed by people; natural evils like earthquakes, floods, and diseases; and imperfections in the normal operations of things. Now, if God were all-powerful and also all good, God would not let these evil things happen. So, it follows that either God is not omnipotent, or God is not entirely good. Either way, the traditional conception of God is undermined.

Philo considers the standard way out of the dilemma, which argues that the evil in the universe is a consequence of the way things must necessarily be set up. Were living creatures incapable of pain, or were animals given a larger repertoire of capacities, or were the universe designed to follow a temperate course, then evil would not exist. But, the defense goes, it was necessary that the universe have the features that allow pain and other limitations. The usual explanation is that these features are necessary to bring about a greater good than otherwise would have been. But, Philo asks, how do we know what is necessary? Our capacities are too limited for this knowledge. It is more reasonable, he argues, to give up the notion that God is good than to think that there is no unnecessary evil. The evidence does not support the opposite conclusion, either--that God is malicious. Rather, given the mixture of pleasure and pain, convenience and trouble, in creation, it is much more likely that the first cause possesses both principles of good and evil or that it is has neither. The first alternative, Philo reasons, is unlikely in view of the stability of the laws of nature, which would probably be in flux if good and evil were set in constant opposition by the first cause. His conclusion, then, is that the first cause is neither good nor evil.

Brief Comments on Philo's and Cleanthes's Conversation

Is it really such a surprise that Hume would have the onlooker, Pamphilus, declare Cleanthes's positions most reasonable at the end of the debate? We know from examining Hume's discussions on other topics that, at times, he sounds like a skeptic, and at other times, he writes like a naturalist giving a positive account of human nature. Supporting Cleanthes represents Hume's naturalist streak. We cannot help but suppose a cause for any effect, and we must infer the nature of the cause from our experience, just as Cleanthes does with the nature of God. Had Cleanthes attempted to support belief in a Deity whose features are unlike anything we know (as Demea contends they are), he would be doing just what Hume warns us we cannot do--say something meaningful about objects beyond experience. But Cleanthes is instead a good empiricist. Of course, his view runs into problems when tested by the orthodox conception of God, but one of Hume's goals is to show us that the orthodox conception has no coherence on empiricist tenets.

At the end, Pamphilus also deems Philo's skeptical position second to that of Cleanthes, but better than the rationalist line of Demea. So, skepticism about the nature of God comes in for some recommendation as well. The spots in which Hume seems to recommend it are just those where Cleanthes's position falters--namely, in articulating the nature of the first cause. We cannot help but believe in a first cause, but we can say little about its nature. Reason indicates that it is a cause with no reference to good and evil, no personal or moral attributes. So perhaps Hume's own view, all things considered, is that it is reasonable to believe in a first cause; but whatever its nature, it is not the personal God of the traditional believer. Many educated people at Hume's time were deists, believing in a God that has no personal interaction with creation. Hume would probably be at home among this group, which included some of the founding fathers of the United States of America, people with whom Hume also had political affinities.

A Future State?

It is also integral to the doctrines of many religions that there be a future state of existence beyond death. This future state is in traditional belief tied to the distribution of justice, with Providence ensuring that goodness is rewarded and evil is punished. Hume is intent, in the second-last section of his *Enquiry Concerning Human Understanding*, on combating the argument that the denial of this future state is a threat to the peace and security of society, as it was charged by many to be. He also wants to show that rationality does not require that we believe in perfect justice.

Hume has his opponents examine the world around them; they will find there a natural system of reward and punishment:

> I acknowledge, that, in the present order of things, virtue is attended with more peace of mind than vice, and meets with a more favourable reception from the world. I never balance between the virtuous and the vicious course of life; but am sensible that, to a well-disposed mind, every advantage is on the side of the former (EHU 140).

Hume wisely notes that regardless of whether one supposes a Deity who has ordered things in this way, or not, it is still incumbent upon human beings to regulate their behavior by experience of past events. If they realize that virtuous behavior makes their lives better than vicious, then it is in their nature to be guided by this belief.

If one argues that there must be perfect distributive justice in the universe, whereby everyone is awarded exactly in proportion to their virtue and punished exactly in proportion to their evil, Hume asks on what such a supposition is based.

> *Are there any marks of a distributive justice in the world?* If you answer in the affirmative, I conclude, that, since justice here exerts itself, it is satisfied. If you reply in the negative, I conclude that you have no good reason to ascribe justice, in our sense of it, to the gods (EHU 141).

We can say nothing of a cause that we have not experienced, so even if the justice of the Deity begins in this world and is fulfilled in the next, we could never know it. Here Hume applies the point that he belabored at great length in the *Dialogues*: the Deity is only known by its effects. Attributes that go beyond what we find in the product are conjecture. All we can know of God's justice is the degree of justice we find here.

Consequently, the argument from distributive justice for a future state is total speculation. Hume himself admitted on his deathbed that he could find no good reason to expect something more. He would be the first to admit that he could be wrong, but a wise person always proportions his belief to the evidence.

Discussion Questions

1. Is Hume right that the credibility of miracles turns on the credibility of testimony?
2. What features of the universe and what features of an organism might lead one to think the former is analogous to the latter?
3. Does Philo have a good argument for claiming that it is more likely that God is neither good nor evil than that God is one or the other?

Endnotes

1. "A Dialogue," in *EHU,* 324-43.

Bibliography

Allenstreet, Richard. *The Whole Duty of Man* (London: printed by R. Norton for Robert Pawlet, 1677).

Baier, Annette. *A Progress of Sentiments: Reflections on Hume's Treatise* (Harvard University Press, 1991).

Birch, Thomas, ed. *The Works of the Honorable Robert Boyle*, 6 vols. (London, 1672).

Blackburn , Simon. *Spreading the Word* (Oxford: Clarendon Press, 1980).

Clarke, Samuel. *A Discourse concerning the Unchangeable Obligations of Natural Religion*. 1706.

Fieser, James. Introduction to "The Essays on Suicide and the Immortality of the Soul" (1783 edition), *The Writings of David Hume*, ed. James Fieser (Internet Release, 1995).

Garrett, Don. *Cognition and Commitment in Hume's Philosophy* (Oxford, 1997).

Grieg, J.Y.T. , ed. *The Letters of David Hume*, 2 vols. (Oxford, 1932).

Hume, David."My Own Life," in *Essays: Moral, Political, and Literary*, ed. Eugene Miller (Indianapolis: Liberty Classics, 1985).

Hutcheson, Francis. *Essay on the Nature of the Passions and Affections. With Illustrations on the Moral Sense* (1728).
   An Inquiry into the Original of our Ideas of Beauty and Virtue; In Two Treatises (1725).

Locke, John. *Essay Concerning Human Understanding* (1689).

Mackie, J.L. *Hume's Moral Theory* (London; Boston: Routledge & Kegan Paul, 1980).

Mossner, E.C. *The Life of David Hume,* 2nd ed. (Oxford: Clarendon Press, 1980).

Stroud, Barry. *Hume* (London: Routledge & Kegan Paul, 1977).

Traiger, Saul."Impressions, Fictions, and Ideas," *Hume Studies* 13 (Nov. 1987): 381-399.

Wood, Paul. "'The Fittest man in the Kingdom': Thomas Reid and the Glasgow Chair of Moral Philosophy," *Hume Studies* XXIII (November 1997): 277-313.